THE PARRYS OF PHILADELPHIA AND NEW HOPE

A Quaker Family's Lasting Impact on Two Historic Towns

ROY ZIEGLER

iUniverse, Inc.
Bloomington

The Parrys of Philadelphia and New Hope
A Quaker Family's Lasting Impact on Two Historic Towns

iUniverse books may be ordered through booksellers or by contacting:

iUniverse
1663 Liberty Drive
Bloomington, IN 47403
www.iuniverse.com
1-800-Authors (1-800-288-4677)

ISBN: 978-1-4502-8579-7 (pbk)
ISBN: 978-1-4502-8581-0 (cloth)
ISBN: 978-1-4502-8580-3 (ebk)

Library of Congress Control Number: 2011900577

Printed in the United States of America

iUniverse rev. date: 2/15/2011

To Dorothy Hillingworth Rosenwald

About the Author

Roy Ziegler is the immediate past president of the New Hope Historical Society. His previous book, *New Hope, Pennsylvania—River Town Passages*, traced three hundred years of New Hope's rich history. As a director of the historical society over the past seven years, Mr. Ziegler has conducted in-depth research into the family members and activities of the Parry family in Philadelphia and New Hope. He has presented lectures and has written numerous articles in local periodicals and newspapers on local history.

Contents

List of Illustrations

Acknowledgments

Special thanks to Charles F. Tarr, Stephen T. Krencicki, Edwin Hild, New Hope Historical Society, Bucks County Historical Society, Historical Society of Pennsylvania, John Carter Brown Library, Lower Merion Historical Society, Philadelphia City Archives, Philadelphia Historical Commission, Philadelphia Museum of Art, PhillyHistory. org, Spruance Library, Temple University Urban Archives, Upper Moreland Historical Association, and Wayne County Historical Society for the information and assistance they provided in the production of this publication.

Introduction

During the first one hundred years of its history, the United States of America blossomed from a hodgepodge of mostly rural agrarian communities into a looming industrial giant that foreshadowed its future role as the only superpower in the world.

Its independence from a freedom-stifling mother country injected a sense of destiny and determination into the collective consciousness of the fledgling nation, a consciousness that nearly disintegrated into fatal chaos during its tragic and disastrous civil war. Emerging slowly and bitterly in fits and starts, the country gradually regained its vision and direction, albeit ever retaining a kind of schizophrenic unity of purpose.

The names leading the way in the unprecedented triumph of independence and enterprise are now familiar to most of the inhabitants of the technologically connected twenty-first-century world community. George Washington, Thomas Jefferson, Benjamin Franklin, Alexander Hamilton, and Abraham Lincoln are the leaders who dominate the world's perception of early America. But the hundreds of individuals and families who helped to form the young nation's work ethic and sense of destiny are unknown to all but a fraction of those who have inherited their legacy. Those were the farmers, inventors, local community leaders, and developers who made the Declaration of Independence a workable and meaningful document by building and strengthening the nation's communities.

This is a story about one Quaker family, who, like so many others, left their homeland to seek a world in which they could practice their religion without ridicule or persecution, and where their hard work, extensive knowledge, skills, and fairness would be justly rewarded. The Parry family from Caernarvonshire, North Wales, in the United

Kingdom, who settled in Bucks County, Pennsylvania, in the middle of the eighteenth century, exemplifies the personal attributes of so many thousands of early settlers that helped to make the United States of America the dominant force in world affairs. This book follows two generations of the Parry family, spanning a period of about one hundred years from the pre-Revolutionary War period to the end of the American Civil War.

Benjamin Parry began his business career in what is now New Hope, Pennsylvania, just about twenty years after the last Native American had left the area. His leadership helped to grow the local economy and eventually catapulted the town into becoming the industrial capital of Bucks County. His patent for machinery that preserved grain, corn, and malt for shipping to overseas markets revolutionized the industry and was used extensively by millers around the young nation. His son, Oliver Parry, who for most of his life had resided in Philadelphia, was a principal developer of the western part of the city known as the Spring Garden Historic District before, during, and after the raging civil war between the states. The Bush Hill Estates section of the Spring Garden neighborhood had been a desolate area that was once the repository of the sick and dying victims of the yellow fever epidemic that had turned the city into a veritable ghost town by the end of the eighteenth century. Today, hundreds of the homes that Oliver Parry constructed and inspired remain as fashionable residences along tree-lined streets that he and his nephew and business partner, Nathaniel Randolph, helped to design and create.

Two generations of the Parry family living in two distinctly different and challenging times calling for steadfast determination and creative industry had a lasting impact on two historic American towns. It is my hope that their stories will help to shed some light on the basic elements of decency, innovation, and hard work that inspired entrepreneurs in the early periods of US history and helped to turn the American dream of the nation's founders into reality.

Roy Ziegler

The Parry Family Coat of Arms

CHAPTER 1
The Parry Heritage

───

Hope, ambition, persistence, and dedication seem to have dominated the Parry family's genetic code. Those strong character traits had an impact on their societies and cultures for centuries. The Parrys boasted a long-standing, honorable lineage beginning in Caernarvonshire, North Wales, in the United Kingdom. The Parry family sprang from those early powerful tribes or clans that existed in North Wales in the twelfth century. Their ranks include magistrates, lieutenants of the county, and a sheriff. Thomas Parry was treasurer to Queen Elizabeth I of England. Lord Richard Parry was Bishop of St. Asaph in 1604. Sir Love P. J. Parry, a member of the British Parliament, was severely wounded and lost a leg at the epic Battle of Waterloo, and Sir Edward Parry was an important Arctic explorer.[1]

The Parry coat of arms vividly depicted them as sportsmen and warriors in ancient times. The crest was a war charger's head with a stag trippant—walking with its right leg raised—on a shield. That was a far cry from the peaceful Quakers who settled in Pennsylvania many centuries later to play their prominent roles in the early development of the two historic towns of Philadelphia and New Hope. The spark that kindled the Parry drive for sport and the battlefield early on in their history continued to drive the family's competitive quest for community leadership and industrial enterprise well into the twentieth century.

Caernarvonshire is located in the northwest corner of Wales and is one of the most beautiful and scenic places in the United Kingdom. It is a land of great castles, lofty headlands, and picturesque valleys along a surging sea. The English biographer Dr. Samuel Johnson once remarked that one of the castles in Wales could contain all of the castles he had seen in Scotland. The county was created in 1284 and was known as Caernarvonshire for nearly eight centuries until it was abolished in 1974 when it became part of the nonmetropolitan county of Gwynedd. Then in 1996 the former territory of Caernarvonshire was divided between the unitary authorities of Gwynedd and Conwy. Today it is known as Gwynedd.[2]

Love Parry's son—Thomas Parry, born in 1680 in Caernarvonshire, North Wales—was the first generation of the Quaker family to settle in the United States. In 1700 he moved to a part of Philadelphia County that is now known as Upper Moreland Township in Montgomery County, Pennsylvania. Thomas Parry, the grandfather of Benjamin Parry, settled in the old Manor of Moreland, in the beautiful Huntingdon Valley. Indeed, the rolling green hills and sparkling waterways of Montgomery County must truly have given the Parry settlers a warm feeling of home when they arrived there more than three centuries ago.

The Parrys were Quakers who sought to leave England because of the increasingly apparent irreconcilable differences that had developed between them and their more traditional Englishmen. The Quakers were plain and simple people but were not tied to old customs. They would not seek religious advice from clergymen and refused to use secular titles. Their belief that God inspired them through direct communication with their inner spirit or light ran contrary to the submission to authority that the Anglican Church had demanded. Even though the Quakers were Christians and did not become members of the Church, they were required to pay taxes to the institution. It is little wonder why so many Quakers strove to leave England for the new land that promised freedom from the authority that they did not recognize and from which they were experiencing growing animosity and persecution. Even the prospect of becoming indentured servants, as many of them were for years until the cost of their transport to America was paid, did not deter them from their inexorable flight to freedom.

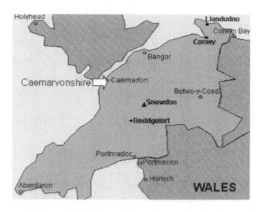

Map of North Wales showing Caernarvonshire
Courtesy of the New Hope Historical Society

King Charles II gave William Penn, a Quaker, the authority to establish vast estates of land that were called "manors" in America as payment for a huge debt that the king had owed to Penn's deceased father. Of the six manors that Penn established, all but one of them were set aside for his family. The exception was the Manor of Moreland. The manor dates back to 1682 when William Penn deeded about ten thousand acres to Dr. Nicholas More for one shilling silver for every one hundred acres, annually, forever. Dr. More was president of the Free Society of Traders, an English land-trading organization, and later Penn appointed Dr. More to be the first chief justice of Pennsylvania.[3]

The Manor of Moreland
After Dr. More's death in 1687, the land was divided and sold. The Manor of Moreland was located on a strip of land in Montgomery County, Pennsylvania, separated by the boundary of Philadelphia County. Visitors to that area are almost certain to be surprised to discover a gigantic, modern shopping complex that includes scores of shops and a Bloomingdale's department store. One can easily imagine the amazement of the members of Dr. More's old Society of Traders if they could see their land today.

Thomas Parry bought about three hundred acres of the Manor of Moreland. He quickly expanded a gristmill on the land in 1731 that Sampson Davis had originally established. It later became known as Morgan's Mill after the Parry family sold it to Benjamin Morgan. Later,

William F. Morgan ran an ice mill there.[4] Interestingly, the land had once been owned by James Cooper, grandfather of the legendary author James Fenimore Cooper, whose book *The Last of the Mohicans* is a classic in early American literature. Thomas Parry eventually owned about one thousand acres of land. Five hundred acres were located in nearby Upper Dublin Township. He sold that land in 1726 and deeded the remaining five hundred acres to his oldest son, Thomas.

Thomas Parry's Gristmill circa 1731
Photograph by Roy Ziegler

Records indicate that a typical mill village called Morganville, consisting of the mill and about ten houses, sprang up around the intersection of Parry's Road (now Davisville Road) and Mill Road (now Terwood Road). In the late twentieth century, Davisville Road became a major four-lane traffic artery connecting Montgomery and Bucks Counties. Today, the location of Parry's old mill is a bustling intersection. The Parrys could never have imagined that, 250 years later, the Pennsylvania Turnpike would carry thousands of gas-powered vehicles at unheard-of speeds high above the road named for them. The modern, sprawling Upper Moreland High School is situated on the edge of what had been for many decades the property of the Parry family. Their mill was located about a half mile from the legendary Old York Road.

Parry-Morgan House (foreground)
Photograph by Roy Ziegler

Unfortunately, the mill that Thomas Parry built and expanded in 1731 was demolished in the 1960s. The site is memorialized by a historic marker that the Upper Moreland Historical Association had placed on the southwest corner of Terwood and Davisville Roads, the location of the original mill. The mill appears on tax records in 1776 indicating that John Parry, Thomas's son, was the owner of 106 acres. A partial wooden drive gear from the mill has survived to the twenty-first century and is currently on display at the Upper Moreland Historical Association. The area had once been known as Round Meadow, but according to the Upper Moreland Historical Association, the name was lost when a cartographer, Reading Howell, while traveling in the vicinity, noticed a man planting willow trees. Howell designated the area on his map as Willow Grove, and the name was permanently established around 1792.

As Thomas Parry was establishing his family and business at the

Manor of Moreland, a new community was forming just twenty miles east that would, two generations later, be dominated by his grandson Benjamin Parry, who would become known as the "father of New Hope." That town's history began when William Penn sold one thousand acres in what is now the borough of New Hope to Robert Heath, with the understanding that Heath would build a corn or flour mill that would become the center of a new town. Heath's son, Richard, fulfilled that promise, and the community now known as New Hope, Pennsylvania, was born. Ironically, neither Robert nor his son, Richard, ever settled in the community they had created. Both father and son continued to live in Bristol Township, Pennsylvania, some thirty miles south of New Hope.

By 1725, the original part of Old York Road that had opened around 1711 was under construction, albeit rough and primitive. It eventually linked Philadelphia to the town that Richard Heath had established. Old York Road was completed between Philadelphia and Wells Ferry (later New Hope) around 1737, and by 1764 it had become a major route between the city of Philadelphia and New York City. A young speculator, John Wells, purchased half of the one thousand acres that Penn had sold to Heath from Heath's heirs, and the town received its first name, "Wells Ferry," in 1715. Wells proceeded to open a ferry boat operation to carry travelers from the Philadelphia area across the Delaware River to continue their trip to New York.

Thomas Parry's son, John, owned and operated the mill at the Manor of Moreland at Round Meadow Run. John's young son, Benjamin Parry, most probably served his apprenticeship there. John Parry was a neighbor and close friend of Dr. Joseph Todd and his wife, Martha. Young Benjamin most probably spent his summers working in Todd's mill learning the business at an early age.

Drive Wheel from Thomas Parry's Mill
Photograph by Roy Ziegler

Dr. and Mrs. Todd moved from Montgomery County to Coryell's Ferry, formerly Wells Ferry, in Bucks County around 1767. Several years later, in 1771, they purchased sixteen acres of farmland in the mill tract and one of the largest gristmills, in what is now the center of the New Hope community. The mill had been constructed by Philip Atkinson in 1763. The purchase included water rights on the Delaware River. When the mill became unmanageable for the ailing Dr. Todd around 1782, John Parry sent Benjamin, then about twenty-five years old, to Coryell's Ferry to help manage it. Within a period of ten years, Benjamin and his brother, Thomas, had acquired the Todds' property and most of what was then known as Coryell's Ferry.

Benjamin Parry had arrived.

Drawing of Benjamin Parry circa 1826
Courtesy of the New Hope Historical Society

CHAPTER 2
Benjamin Parry, Father of New Hope

B y the time that Benjamin Parry first set foot in what is now New Hope, Pennsylvania, around 1782 with his brothers, Thomas and Daniel, the gritty little town was already into its third generation and had been known by three different names. It was common in those times for towns to be named for the person who owned the major industry.

After Richard Heath's death in 1717, Thomas Canby and his Philadelphia partners purchased the old Heath Mill and nearly half of the town's one thousand acres. Canby was a strong-willed, active entrepreneur and a newly elected member of the Pennsylvania Assembly. He had been an early ferryman who operated Baker's Ferry that later in the nation's history would serve as the site of General George Washington's epic crossing of the Delaware River. The village, then known as McConkey's Ferry, is now Washington Crossing, Pennsylvania, and is located just seven miles south of New Hope. But with all of his drive and influence, Thomas Canby failed in his long and bitter struggle with John Wells to purchase the ferry site along the Delaware River in the town that is known today as New Hope.[5]

John Wells, a carpenter from Lower Dublin Township, Pennsylvania, had purchased another large portion of the town's one thousand acres from the heirs of Richard Heath. In 1719 he obtained a license from the province of Pennsylvania to operate a ferry across the Delaware River and to establish the first inn. He became the first recorded person to hold rights to operate a ferry on the Pennsylvania side of the Delaware River, and the town of Wells Ferry was born.

Wells was prominent in the fight to have Old York Road in Philadelphia redirected from its original terminus at Reading's Ferry in what is now Center Bridge to its new destination at Wells Ferry. The horses that drew the heavily laden carriages no doubt had the winning argument, since the steep hills out of Reading's Ferry were taking their toll on the dependable but not indestructible animals. The change in the direction of Old York Road vastly advanced the development of Wells Ferry. The Ferry House, built by Wells in 1727, continues to host travelers and local residents today as the Logan Inn more than 275 years later. Wells also served as justice of the peace for ten years.

Wells befriended a young lad, William Kitchen, an unemployed and distraught weaver by trade, whom he had met along a roadside in his travels around Bucks County. Kitchen later married Wells's niece, Rebecca Norton. Kitchen became a very important part of Wells's business operations, and he and his young bride moved in with John Wells. Kitchen later purchased a parcel of land from his mentor along the Delaware River near the ferry operation, where he built his first home.

When the opportunity arose in 1748, Benjamin Canby, Thomas's son, wasted no time purchasing the ferry and the inn in addition to one hundred acres from John Wells, thereby avenging one of the few unsuccessful business ventures that his celebrated father had experienced. Canby also constructed one of the first iron forges in the area on a ten-acre lot that he had also purchased from Wells's family. Benjamin Canby operated the ferry in what became known as Canby's Ferry for the next twenty years until it was purchased by John Coryell and became known as Coryell's Ferry, Pennsylvania.

John Coryell was one of the most colorful figures in the town's early history. In the early 1700s his father, Emmanuel Coryell, perceived the growing value of the area now known as Lambertville, New Jersey, located directly across the Delaware River from the fledgling Wells Ferry. He purchased land along the old Indian trails leading from New York City to the Delaware River. There he developed his ferry operations between New Jersey and Pennsylvania. His town became known as Coryell's Ferry, New Jersey.

Emmanuel had a very short life and died before he was fifty years old. He left real estate totaling about 1,500 acres. John Coryell, with the help of his father's inheritance, eventually purchased the ferry operations that had originally been established by John Wells across the Delaware River in Pennsylvania.

In 1764, about twenty-two years before Benjamin Parry's arrival, New Hope, Pennsylvania, and Lambertville, New Jersey, both bore the name "Coryell's Ferry" and maintained that name for nearly forty years.

John Coryell was well regarded by most local residents and was a shrewd businessman. However, he was known to have kept slaves, contrary to the Quaker tradition that prevailed in the community. He was a true patriot and strong supporter of General George Washington. Coryell responded to the growing demand for transportation across the Delaware River to New Jersey. He built the largest ferryboat known in the region to accommodate the increased traffic emanating from Lancaster County in the western part of Pennsylvania. Edwin Tunis writes that the boat was sixty feet long to enable it to carry the Conestoga wagons that had been built by the German farmers from the Lancaster County region. The huge wagons with their teams of six horses could be loaded directly onto the ferryboat for the crossing. Eventually in February 1788, John Beaumont purchased seventy-two acres of his land, including his buildings, ferries, and landing, in a sheriff sale.

Benjamin Parry Begins His Career in New Hope

Dr. Joseph Todd died in 1776, leaving his widow and two young sons to oversee the management of their properties. Benjamin Parry and his older brother Thomas, who had been assisting the Todds in the operation of their mills, did not hesitate to seize the opportunity when the widow Todd decided to sell the property. The agreement to sell to the Parrys was executed in 1785. As with most transactions in that time period, the deed to the property was transferred years later in 1789. In that same year, John Parry, the father of Benjamin and Thomas, passed away. It seems probable that his sons were able to purchase the property at least in part from their inheritance.[6]

Benjamin Parry, a promising twenty-eight-year-old entrepreneur with financial backing from an inheritance from his late father and with the help of his brothers, saw a small, gritty town that had all of the characteristics of what today's economists would call "green shoots" ready for development. There was a tavern, the center of the transportation hub, which served as a kind of town center where folks caught up on the local gossip and news. The gristmill produced flour from grain that was grown by the area's farmers. The ferry crossing, although busy, had not yet reached its great potential. Coryell's Ferry was also a popular layover location for the Durham boats carrying iron from the nearby Durham furnace to the towns along the Delaware River. Local farmers brought their produce and farm animals there to be loaded onto Durham boats for shipping downriver to the city of Philadelphia.

The general store provided basic dry goods and food for the small population. The salt store supplied the all-important preservative for food supplies. The sawmill was beginning to increase its production of lumber for the growing community, and a rolling and slitting mill flattened and stretched iron bars, cut them, and produced long nail rods. This production created jobs for local blacksmiths who would make nails by cutting the rods, pointing them, and finishing the job by beating the top of the nails creating large heads.

All these activities were centrally located and surrounded by many hundreds of acres of rich farmland that produced nearly twice as much grain per acre as the soil in the farmers' estranged homeland had yielded. Indeed, Parry family records note that Benjamin owned several farms himself; one was located on twenty-two acres on Goat Hill in Lambertville, New Jersey, just below the Ely family's property.

In nearby Amwell Township, New Jersey, Benjamin purchased from his brother, Daniel Parry, about one hundred acres near the former gristmill of Benjamin Smith. In 1846, the New Jersey legislature split Amwell Township, creating East and West Amwell Townships. Portions of Amwell Township were taken to form Lambertville, New Jersey, in 1849. Benjamin purchased a share in the ownership of the Holcombe Island Fishery on the Delaware River and bought one-fourth of the Malta Island nearby and land that later became the site of the Union Mills in New Hope. Malta Island gained prominence in the history of the American Revolutionary War when it became the place where Durham boats were sequestered for the famous crossing of the Delaware

River on Christmas night, 1776. That night, led by General George Washington, his army turned the course of the war at the strategically important Battle of Trenton.

New Hope was the halfway point on the journey from Philadelphia to New York City at the time. In her publication, "Architectural Patterns in an Early River Town," Margaret Bye Richie noted that "New Hope with its ample supply of amenities was now to rank among the more prosperous villages in the Delaware Valley. It had grown steadily." There were three main roads in the town. Old York Road connected the town with Philadelphia and New York City. River Road ran along the Delaware River in front of the gristmill and across the milldam to Mechanic Street. That was the old road that led from the center of the town to the old Heath Mill about one mile to the west.[7] The third road, Sugan Road, connected local farms with New Hope and was a major route for transporting wheat and corn from the farms to the mills in the New Hope area.

Benjamin Parry's expanded involvement in the community began when, in 1786, he and Thomas agreed to purchase an old frame building located at the edge of the Todds' mill property. It was one of the oldest general stores in Bucks County. Daniel Parry operated the store, which supplied dry goods, produce, and meats from the Parry farms to millworkers and residents of the small village. Three years later in 1789, Martha Todd and her sons, Charles and William, sold their sixteen acres, including the mills and dam, to the Parry brothers.

Daniel Parry became a wandering speculator whose financial exploits led him far beyond Philadelphia and New Hope. He was a gentleman of fortune who owned large tracts of land in Bradford, Carbon, Luzerne, and Wayne Counties in Pennsylvania. Benjamin had assisted Daniel with his financial matters in 1814 when he agreed to sell part of his Prime Hope Mills property in Titusville, New Jersey, just across the Delaware River from his New Hope Mills. The sale helped his brother liquidate some of his debts. Daniel had purchased land in Asylum, Pennsylvania, from Robert Morris of Philadelphia and from the Marquis de Noailles of France, who was the Marquis de Lafayette's brother-in-law. The settlement, in the southeastern section of Bradford County, Pennsylvania, was so named because it was established to provide asylum for French refugees from the French Revolution. Robert

Morris's Asylum Company incorporated his vision that would convert the Susquehanna River into an avenue of commerce, which would link Baltimore to the Great Lakes and the Mississippi River.

Unfortunately for Daniel Parry and to the dismay of many other investors, the financial bankruptcy of Robert Morris and his partner, John Nicholson, and the subsequent loss of most of their property doomed the plan. Robert Morris, a great financier of the American Revolution and a signer of the Declaration of Independence, ended up in debtors' prison. The final blow to the Asylum enterprise was the news that the new emperor, Napoleon Bonaparte, had invited all French emigrants to return home with a promise to restore the ownership of their land. Hearing the news, the Frenchmen were jubilant. "Men hugged and kissed each other to the profound astonishment of American beholders. Some days were spent in feasting and then most of them commenced making preparations to leave Pennsylvania woods for their beloved France."[8] Today there are about 1,100 residents of Asylum, Pennsylvania, including few, if any, French inhabitants.

Daniel Parry was far more successful with his investment in Carbon County. It was a very important point, located south of Jim Thorpe, Pennsylvania, for the shipment of coal south to New Hope and on to Philadelphia. The town of Parryville in Carbon County, Pennsylvania, was named for Daniel Parry. In 2009, Parryville included about five hundred residents, and the median age was just over forty years old.

Through a partnership with Lewis S. Coryell, a leading New Hope entrepreneur, Daniel Parry purchased 2,065 acres of timberland along the Lackawaxen River in Wayne County, Pennsylvania. Daniel Parry and Company established two sawmills that cut more than a million feet of lumber each year. One of the mills was located in White Mills, Pennsylvania. The first settler recorded as living there was Cornelius Coryell, Lewis's father. Parry, however, had never lived in White Mills but had hired Enos Woodward to manage and expand his mill operations. Parry sold the mill property about thirty years later.[9] The continued rapid growth of the cities of Philadelphia and New York created an insatiable need for lumber, coal, and stone to advance the construction of homes and commercial properties in America's first cities. The Delaware and Hudson Canal was built to facilitate the shipping of lumber and anthracite coal from Wayne County when ground transportation was simply too inefficient and cumbersome to haul the vast quantities of commodities that were so desperately needed in the cities. The canal was linked to the Gravity Railroad near Honesdale, Pennsylvania, and extended about 108 miles to the Hudson River in New York State. The construction of the Delaware and Hudson Canal created a dispute between the canal company and the partners, Parry and Coryell, because it originally deprived their sawmills of the required volume of water that was needed to operate them. Today the Lackawaxen River watershed provides water, electricity, and recreation, and the richness of its territory harbors a vast treasure of wildlife and vegetation. In 2010, the Lackawaxen River was honored as the "Pennsylvania River of the Year."

Daniel, like Benjamin, was a very loving and affectionate husband and father. He had only one son, John, who died in infancy. After Daniel's death, a tiny half-worn shoe that had belonged to his infant son was found among his possessions. His loving and faithful heart treasured it for half a century after the baby's tragic death.

The Parry Mansion in 1960
Courtesy of the New Hope Historical Society

Benjamin Parry bought Thomas's half interest in the New Hope general store in 1791. More than two hundred years later, that property continues its commercial success as one of the most popular bookshops in Bucks County. Almost immediately Parry set out to expand the mill operations. He hired his cousin, Jesse Betts, to rebuild the milldam next to the gristmill. Then, he added a lumber mill and flaxseed oil mill and enlarged the gristmill.[10] He soon boasted—in all humility, of course—that he was producing three hundred bushels of flour each week and that his sawmill cut one thousand board feet of lumber each day. Parry had access to a large tract of land located at the mouth of the Lehigh River near Easton, Pennsylvania, where he had harvested the lumber for his mill. Parry family records show that as early as October 1786 he and Thomas had received an order for one thousand feet of weatherboard from a local entrepreneur who had already established an account with the Parrys.

Fire Destroys Parry's Mills

Many of the town's residents and some folks from surrounding communities found their livelihood working in one or another of Parry's mills. The town was growing and prospering. But on one fateful evening in 1790, disaster struck. The gristmill and an adjacent oil mill caught fire and burned to the ground, consuming with them the jobs of the townsfolk who relied on them for their financial sustenance. Millworkers, mechanics, suppliers, laborers, haulers, and blacksmiths faced the dismal prospect of unemployment and economic uncertainty.

Parry was undaunted. His Quaker hope, optimism, and persistence had been instilled in him by his father from the time that he had worked in his father's mills. Those characteristics drove him to have his mills rebuilt quickly. Parry hired his neighbor, Joshua Vansant, who lived across the Aquetong Creek on West Mechanic Street in what is now the oldest house in New Hope. He completed construction of those mills within one year, bringing back prosperity to the town.

In a triumphant gesture of success over adversity, Parry had the words "New Hope Mills" painted on the front of the newly resurrected gristmill. And that sentiment of optimism pervades the town until this day. Gradually, visitors and residents began referring to "New Hope" when they spoke about Coryell's Ferry, and in 1837 the borough of New

Hope was officially incorporated, giving the town its fourth and, most probably, final name. Parry lived to congratulate his nephew, John C. Parry, as he became the first burgess or mayor of New Hope in that year.

Parry's New Hope Mills continued to operate for nearly one hundred years after the borough of New Hope was incorporated. In 1939, a part of the mill was incorporated into the construction of the new Bucks County Playhouse that was founded by a group of local residents and friends from New York City. The original seats for the legendary playhouse were purchased from the owner of a movie theater in Philadelphia that had recently closed.[11] They were shipped from Philadelphia, arriving in New Hope to be installed just hours before the curtain was raised on opening night, July 1, 1939.

Samuel D. Ingham

Benjamin Parry had never been directly involved in politics, and he had never held any political office himself. But he became a close friend and business associate of Samuel D. Ingham, who lived just one mile south of Parry on Old York Road in what is now Solebury Township. Ingham was a member of the Pennsylvania House of Representatives from 1806 to 1808 and was a three-term congressman allied to the John C. Calhoun faction of the Democratic Party. However, it is clear that Ingham did not share Calhoun's political philosophy regarding nullification. Ingham served in Congress from 1813 to 1818 and again from 1822 to 1829.

When Andrew Jackson was elected president in 1829, he tapped Samuel Ingham for the post of secretary of the treasury of the United States. This was seen as a gesture to appease the Calhounites in the party who were still embittered by Jackson's election.[12] Calhoun was known to have desired the presidency, but he was well aware that his chances to obtain that high office were slim. Now he was to become vice president for the second time, having served in that office under President John Quincy Adams. Like the proverbial bridesmaid who never becomes the bride, Calhoun was at times bitter, listless, and disillusioned. He stood for pro-slavery, states' rights, and limited government. At any rate, Ingham's term as treasurer was short-lived. He resigned in 1831, with other members of the cabinet in apparent outrage over the Petticoat affair scandal that had embarrassed the Jackson administration.

From the late 1780s until the mid-1830s, Samuel Ingham continued his involvement and support of Benjamin Parry's numerous business enterprises. Through Ingham, Parry had obtained the water rights to the Aquetong Creek, whose three million gallons of water flowing through the town each day powered his mills. The water rights included the area one mile inland from the Delaware River and one mile north and south along the river. This gave Parry access to the river where massive amounts of cobblestones that had been formed during the glacial period were at the time desperately needed by Philadelphia as the city began building its streets.

18 Strawberry Alley in 2010
Photograph by Stephen T. Krencicki

The Founding of the Bridge Company and Bank

As Parry's business continued to expand, he undoubtedly had thought about the growing cost and delays involved in shipping his goods by ferryboat across the Delaware River to New Jersey and on to New York. In the early part of 1809, Parry began discussions about the prospect of alternative shipping arrangements with his friend Samuel Ingham. The Inghams and the Parrys appear to have been close friends. Ingham's wife, Lydia, had sewn a beautiful sampler that she presented to the Parrys for their home. The colorful sampler is still displayed in the Parry Mansion today. In March 1809, Mr. Ingham filed the following request to Joex Tooo, Esq., member of the House of Representatives in Lancaster, Pennsylvania. It offers an eloquent request for the approval of a law to build the bridge across the Delaware River and provides a comprehensive description of the growing industry that was occurring in the town. It also shows how active Mr. Ingham had been with other clients in the area. (Ingham was not serving in any official government capacity when he wrote this request.)

> Dear Sir:
>
> I beg leave to introduce to your acquaintance my friend, Benjamin Parry. He is the bearer of Petitions from a number of reputable inhabitants from this quarter for a Law to incorporate a company to erect a toll Bridge across the Delaware at New Hope or Coryell's Ferry—we are of opinion that a work of this kind may be effected without difficulty. As numerous mills in the vicinity will keep up a constant intercourse which in our opinion will amplify the undertaking—there are no less than 8 run of grist mill stones, 7 Sawmills, 2 oil mills, a paper mill, a fulling mill besides two pairs of wool carding machines and a woolen factory now erecting all within 2 miles of the ferry and on or at the road leading to it.—in addition to this are 2 nourishing villages on the banks of the river and a daily stage passing between Philadelphia and New York. You have no doubt observed a similar Application for Mitchell's Ferry, which Petition I have signed, and we wish it to be distinctly understood that this application is

not in opposition to that but entirely independent of it—if the people interested in that place and their friends are willing to build a Bridge, I see no reason why they should not be permitted to do so, we therefore do not ask the privilege to their exclusion and should the law be granted to both we shall progress with the work whether they do or not—You will readily perceive that the advantages to be derived to the numerous establishments above mentioned and those to the public, by the erection of Bridge across the river at New Hope, the extensive aid which it would receive from the surplus wealth of interested people near the place, besides that expected from the stage proprietors, and others interested on the road from Philadelphia to New York—If you should think well of our application, your aid in passing the Law will be gratefully considered by your friend and humble servant,

Samuel D. Ingham
6th March 1809[13]

Not surprisingly, the act was passed by the Pennsylvania legislature, allowing Benjamin Parry and his partner, Samuel D. Ingham, to build the bridge across the Delaware River between New Hope, Pennsylvania, and Lambertville, New Jersey. Benjamin Parry was the original promoter of the bridge project. He was the chairman of its first board of managers and he was the first to sign a financial commitment to its construction. He invested $7,200 in the bridge company in 1811. His brother, Daniel Parry, was the treasurer. Benjamin's friend Samuel Ingham became the second subscriber and later was named the first president of the bank that was licensed with the bridge company. Joining them and a number of prominent local businessmen in the bridge company venture was Commodore Charles Stewart, United States Navy, and commander of the great ship, the *Constitution*.

Official construction of the covered wooden bridge that consisted of six spans extending just over a thousand feet commenced on December 28, 1812, and was completed on September 13, 1814. The cost of the bridge was about $68,000.[14] Earlier Parry had bought the rights to the ferry operations, and when the toll bridge across the Delaware River was opened, he shut down the ferry, thus giving him and his partners control of the river crossing at New Hope. Now, no longer did Parry have to pay the ferry operators for shipping his goods to expanded markets, but he and his partners could reap the benefits of their investment by charging others for crossing their bridge.

The construction of the bridge to New Jersey was the single most important development in New Hope in nearly a century. Not since the redirection of Old York Road from Philadelphia to New Hope from its original destination in Center Bridge had the town seen such a dramatic transition. Increased commerce and travel through the community at the beginning of the Industrial Revolution brought new prosperity. Travel between Philadelphia and New York was vastly improved by the elimination of ferryboats. Those revered, albeit travel-restricting relics were replaced with a new, sprawling span that extended across the Delaware River. Parry's dream was fulfilled, and the new bridge immediately afforded a dramatically improved, far more convenient, and swifter passage between the two bustling towns of New Hope and Lambertville to New York City.

The following excerpt from a poem found in the papers of Richard Randolph Parry, written by an unknown early traveler, shows how there has been little change in the attitudes and conduct of drivers over the past two centuries, be they riders of horse-driven carriages of the early nineteenth century or drivers of twenty-first-century gas-powered vehicles:

> The bridges are long and narrow and dark,
> With drive-ways numbering two,
> And you will see on the end of the bridge,
> If you look before passing through;
> This warning printed on a dark background,
> In letters large and white,
> "Beware of too fast driving",
> And this other—"Keep to the right."
>
> Part of the crowd that crosses the bridge,
> Heed not the painted sign,

Admonishing them to "keep to the right"
Or "pay the regular fine."
But learn to their cost ere the bridge is crossed,
That we must reap what'ere we sow,
And it echoes the tread of a countless throng,
Whose hearts are filled with woe.

Both towns, each at the halfway point in the trip between America's first great cities, soon developed new accommodations and amenities for the increasing numbers of travelers. Just twenty-seven years later, the flood of 1841, the most devastating ever known up to that point in history, destroyed the bridge. It was rebuilt and continued to serve the two communities and their visitors until the twentieth century. When it was destroyed again in 1903, Benjamin Parry's grandson, Richard Randolph Parry, was president of the New Hope Delaware Bridge Company. He led the discussions that resulted in the construction of an iron superstructure that was erected on the original piers of the bridge. The *Newtown Enterprise* newspaper reported that the company had a surplus of $20,000 at the time of the devastating flood.

The United States of America,

To all to whom these Letters Patent shall come:

Whereas *Benjamin Parry a Citizen of the United States, hath alleged that he has invented a new and useful improvement being a Machine for drying Corn & Grain of all kinds, and also for drying Malt, meal, & other Substances*

which improvement he states has not been known or used before his application; has affirmed that he does verily believe that he is the true inventor or discoverer of the said improvement,

has paid into the treasury of the United States, the sum of thirty dollars, delivered a receipt for the same, and presented a petition to the Secretary of State, signifying a desire of obtaining an exclusive property in the said improvement, and praying that a patent may be granted for that purpose: **These are therefore** *to grant, according to law, to the said Benjamin Parry his heirs, administrators, or assigns, for the term of fourteen years, from the seventh day of July 1810 the full and exclusive right and liberty of making, constructing, using, and vending to others to be used, the said improvement; a description whereof is given in the words of the said Benjamin Parry himself, in the schedule hereto annexed, and is made a part of these presents.*

In testimony whereof, I have caused these Letters to be made Patent, and the Seal of the United States to be hereunto affixed.

GIVEN under my hand, at the city of Washington, this seventh day of July in the year of our Lord, one thousand eight hundred and ten and of the independence of the United States of America, the thirty fifth

James Madison

BY THE PRESIDENT.

R Smith
Secretary of State.

City of Washington, To wit:

I DO HEREBY CERTIFY, That the foregoing Letters Patent, were delivered to me on the seventh day of July in the year of our Lord, one thousand eight hundred and ten to be examined; that I have examined the same, and find them conformable to law: and I do hereby return the same to the Secretary of State, within fifteen days from the date aforesaid, to wit:—On this seventh day of July in the year aforesaid.

C A Rodney Attorney General of the United States.

The Parry Patent
Courtesy of the New Hope Historical Society

The Parry Patent

While all of the frenetic activity was taking place to lay the groundwork for the authorization of the bridge, Parry continued work on his invention of a process for drying grain and other substances so that they could be shipped to overseas ports without spoiling from excessive heat and moisture during the long journey to tropical ports. He became one of the first proponents of fuel conservation when he advertised his invention as requiring less fuel to be consumed and thereby reducing the danger of fire. His patent for the invention helped to increase his wealth early on. Parry's invention significantly increased his large and lucrative trade with the West Indies. The high quality of the grain that he produced created great demand in a number of foreign countries.

Parry's patent had a wider use. Parry describes the machinery and process that he had invented in his own words on his patent application:[15]

> This machine is intended for the use of flour and corn mills, and brewing and may be erected or attached thereto and the necessary motion communicated either by the water or wind which turns the mill or otherwise according to the circumstances and the wishes of the constructor. It may be considered as composed of the casing or enclosure, the machinery for communicating motion, the drying sieves or furnace oven or stove.
>
> The exterior case or enclosure of the drying apparatus may be composed of walls of brick or stone and other materials which shall confine the heat, and be but little liable to accident from fire. Near the upper part of the case or enclosure and within it, but towards one side a long sieve is suspended by four chains, two of which are near the middle and the other two near the lower or farther end, one end of it projects beyond the outer wall, and from a spout receives the grain, malt or other substance to be dried. This sieve is made of sheet iron or other metal, and perforated with holes for the admission of heated air to the grain. The chains from which it is hung permit the sieve to have a pendulum like motion. This sieve extends nearly the length

of the case or dying chamber and has a gentle descent from the end where it receives the grain to the opposite end.

The grain after passing along this receiving sieve falls over the lower end into another small sieve which extends across the chamber, and carries the grain to the third sieve which extends the length of the chamber parallel to the first and discharges the dried grain at the end where it is first received. This cross sieve is also hung with chain so as to receive a swinging motion, and has a small descent from the lower end of the first long sieve, to the upper end of the long sieve by which the grain is returned. From the lower end of the cross sieve, the grain falls on the returning sieve which has a small descent to where it issues from the drying case or chamber, where it discharges the dried grain. It hangs on chains so as to have a swinging motion similar to the sieve last above described. Beneath these sieves and within the chamber or enclosure for the heat, in which the sieves are placed, is a stove, oven or furnace framed with metal or other plates or with metal and some other substance which will bear the action of the fires the fuel is introduced by the opening or door in one of the side or end walls of the chamber; and the smoke carried off by a flue or pipe, with proper dampers or registers for regulating the heat.

On the outside of the case or walls that enclose the drying chamber there extends an horizontal shaft which receives a rotary motion from the mill or moving power. This shaft has two projecting cams or teeth which by striking against projected pieces from the ends of the long sieves gives them sufficient motion to cause the grain to progress along them.

There is a small cog wheel on this shaft, which acts on another cog wheel on the end of a shaft which extends nearly horizontally through the drying chamber under the first sieve, and by a projecting tooth or cam at or near its opposite and gives motion to the transverse sieve which conveys the grain from the lower end of the receiving to the upper end of the discharging sieve. In order to give a jar or jerking motion to the sieve there are bows of metal or springs at the side which, by striking against some freed part of the machine produce this effect. The stove or oven may be of any convenient form or materials and so tight as not to admit the smoke to escape and injure the grain.

President James Madison signed Benjamin Parry's patent, and it was issued to Parry on July 7, 1810.

On July 30, 1810, Benjamin Parry began announcing his new invention in newspapers around the young nation with the following advertisement:

TO THE MILLERS IN THE U. STATES—The subscriber living in the village of New Hope, in the county of Bucks, and state of Pennsylvania, having invented machinery for drying corn, malt and other substances, which in its operations dries the grain completely, without any manual labor, and requires much less fuel than the usual method; there is also less danger of accident by fire, and the grain is more uniformly dried than by any other process heretofore made use of, —for which the subscriber has obtained a Patent-right, granting him the full and exclusive right and liberty of making, constructing, using, and vending to others to be used, the said Improvement.—Those persons who may think proper to avail themselves of said Improvement, may see it in operation at his mills in New Hope; which, on inspection, he is fully of the opinion will be approved by them—or where the distance will not admit of a view of it, a specification and description will be sent, if advised.

BENJAMIN PARRY
July 30, 1810

Parry's marketing effort got quick results. Just about a year and a half later the following announcement appeared in Fredericksburg, Virginia:

We do hereby certify, that we have erected one of Parry's kiln-dryers, which we find from experience superior to anything of the kind yet discovered for drying corn … 500 bushels of corn in 24 hours, sufficiently dry to ship or grind for exportation; and will not consume more than half a cord of wood if fires are properly attended to, in twenty-four hours.

Howard & Lawrence
Fredericksburg, Virginia
January 21, 1812

There is evidence that Parry's patent continued to provide income over the years. A copy of a license shows that he had received a payment of seventy-five dollars from Samuel Penny of New York City for use in his mills in Morris County, New Jersey, on February 4, 1818. In today's economy, the fee for each license would equate to approximately $1,300.

The well-respected local engineer and entrepreneur, Lewis S. Coryell, is said to have written that the reputation of the grain so treated was so great "that the amount of production was the only limit for the demand for the article in foreign parts."[16]

The original patent document that was granted to Benjamin Parry in 1810 was destroyed in a sweeping fire that also burned about ten thousand other patents in 1836 in Washington DC. They had ironically been placed in temporary storage while a new, more fireproof facility was under construction. Incredibly, a fire station was located next to the patent storage building but was unable to prevent the fire because the company's hoses and pumps had frozen in the winter weather. Fortunately, in 2006, the New Hope Historical Society's diligent and persistent search discovered the original patent that had been issued to Parry by President Madison with its original seal from 1810 still attached at the Bucks County Historical Society's Spruance Library. A copy was presented to the United States Patent Office for the federal government's records at that time.[17]

A Twenty-First-Century Grain Dryer
Courtesy of Matthews Company

The photograph of the twenty-first-century version of Benjamin Parry's original chain-driven grain dryer that is included in this publication shows how Parry's process has endured and has morphed into our modern technological system. It is a poignant illustration of the influence and creativity of one of our early American entrepreneurs and inventors who helped to lead the way in the industrial development of the nation.

As he gained greater insight into the operation of the gristmill, Parry continued to work to increase its effectiveness and production. Thomas P. Cope was an early visitor to Parry's mill and attested to Parry's business acumen in his diary. Cope was a merchant apprentice who later made a fortune sending ships from Philadelphia to Europe and Asia. A city councilman in Philadelphia, he was charged with the responsibility of introducing a public water supply to the city. Toward the end of his life he became a principal organizer of the Pennsylvania Railroad.

In his diary, Cope wrote that he visited New Hope on September 4, 1813, where he noted that a bridge on stone piers was being built over the Delaware River. That night he wrote, "At Parry's mill I saw for the first time that a blower for forcing meal, as a substitute for the Evans

Elevator. He [Parry] also has some small horizontal water wheels, on a new construction, the principal benefit of which appears to be in the smallness of the space they occupy."[18]

By 1816 Parry was leasing his saw and oil mills to New Hope's great entrepreneur, Lewis S. Coryell, for five hundred dollars a year while retaining the right for himself to use as much water with any and all of the gristmill wheels as he would think proper. While Benjamin continued to use his mills, he earned additional income for renting them to Coryell. Parry also leased several homes that he and his brothers had built in New Hope.

Benjamin Parry, Husband

With all of the drive and energy that he needed to operate and expand his businesses, Parry continued to be a thoughtful and loving husband to Jane Paxson Parry, whom he had married in 1787 at the Buckingham Friends Meeting House. While in the throes of his new responsibilities for his recently acquired mills and properties, Parry, nonetheless, lavished his attention on the love of his life.

Jane Paxson was the daughter of Oliver Paxson, a prominent farmer and businessman in the community. He owned several hundred acres of land on the north side of town that is currently the site of the New Hope-Solebury High School and the Union Square commercial district. Paxson also operated the important salt store and leased the property from his son-in-law, Benjamin Parry. Jane was a descendent of Mary Oliver, whose parents had come to America on the ship *Welcome* with William Penn in 1684.

It is not known how Benjamin and Jenny, Jane's pet name, had met. Jane's father operated the town's salt store that was located on property that was owned by Benjamin in what is now a fine Northern Italian restaurant offering the cozy ambience of a massive eighteenth-century fireplace. Paxson's store was located next door to Parry's general store that he and his brother, Daniel, had operated at the time. Perhaps they had met at her father's salt store or at Benjamin's general store, or maybe they had met at the Buckingham Friends Meeting House.

Jane had resided at her home at Maple Grove on the Paxson estate, now known as the Rhoads estate, which is one of the oldest homes in the area. When Jane was about eleven years old her parents hosted two very important guests. George and Martha Washington stayed with the Paxsons one evening in June 1778 when General Washington led the Continental Army from Valley Forge to the Battle of Monmouth. The army crossed the Delaware River at Coryell's Ferry over a period of two nights and three days. An amusing story is told of General Washington's response to Mrs. Washington when she asked him what she should do, if she would encounter the flirtatious General Howe. George is said to have quipped that Martha should wear one of Mrs. Paxson's Quaker dresses, and she would be completely safe from Howe's advances.

Jane Paxson's home was located directly across Old York Road from property that Benjamin owned. Maybe they met among the maples that lined the road leading to her father's estate. However they may have met, it is clear that Benjamin and Jane were very much in love. Benjamin wrote an acrostic poem to Jane a couple of years before they were married. He used each letter of Jane Paxson's name as the first letter of each line in the love poem. He took a bit of poetic license when he started the poem, with the letter "I" substituting for the letter "J." But the rest of the poem is true to form. It reads as follows:

Inform me, Shepherds of the green, where roves my lovely maiden?
Enamored with the birds that sing, thee's sought some pleasant shade.
Not blooming meads, or golden fields, was ever half so fair.
Nor May with all her fragrant flowers, did e're so bright appear.
Young as the morning, her blushes far more clear
Pure as the morning dew, her breath that blows the fragrant flowers,
And ruby lips, a saint might kiss, or infidel adore.
Xenophen wise who scoft at love, and mocked the lovers' pains,
Saw never half so fair a maid, or had owned young cupids chains.
O'er hoary mountain tops I'd glide, from forests; leaves I'd tear,
Nor bars of steels obstruct my way, to keep one from my fair.[19]

That lovely, romantic poem was written by a young man who had just taken control of one of the largest mill operations in the area and was negotiating to purchase additional properties while planning to build his home. The descriptions that Parry used in his writing may well have been inspired by the beautiful Manor of Moreland, where he was born and spent his youth.

And the romance was clearly two-sided. A few years after their marriage, Jane wrote to Benjamin while she was visiting relatives in Philadelphia:

> Once more, my dear, is thy poor wife left alone, and who can she speak to or think of but her best beloved, who, indeed, is ever in my remembrance ... Two weeks is a long time when separated from those we dearly love and in whose welfare we are so deeply interested. As I am thine; I do so long to see thee once more. Give my love to our father's family... Reserve a large share of that love which has ever subsisted between us, for thy own dear self.
>
> From thy affectionate wife, Jane
> June 28, 1790

It is clear that Jane Parry had taken good care to make sure that her loving and hardworking husband was well nourished. The *Quaker Lady's Cookbook,* which has been preserved by the New Hope Historical Society, includes a number of delectable recipes that Jane used to prepare meals for Benjamin after a hard day's journey home from his Philadelphia business or from his trips back from his New Jersey mill operations or from the challenging days tending to his various enterprises in Coryell's Ferry.

One can imagine Benjamin returning home to his Georgian-style mansion for a nourishing dinner of pickled oysters, potted beef with cloves and rock salt that had been marinating for fifteen days and then baked carefully with finely chopped suet covered with a delicious paste, and then potato pudding made with butter, sugar, eggs, cream, wine, and spice. Jane would prepare a special dessert of almond sponge cake made with ten egg yolks, one pound of sugar, two handfuls of almonds, a glass of rosewater, egg whites, and flour. Or, on other occasions, Benjamin would be treated to a whip syllabub made with a half pint of cream, a half pint of wine, a pound of sugar, and the juice of a lemon, and then whipped with four egg whites.

Benjamin and Jane brought four children into the late-eighteenth- and early-nineteenth-century world of Coryell's Ferry. His son, Oliver, would build upon Benjamin's dazzling reputation as an entrepreneur of great character and expertise. Oliver would become one of the most important community developers in the city of Philadelphia in the early nineteenth century. Two of their daughters, Jane and Ruth, never married. Benjamin's daughter Margaret married Charles Knowles of Brownsburg, Pennsylvania, a small village that is located just a few miles south of New Hope. Knowles became prominent in New Hope when he owned and operated the soap factory there in the early part of the nineteenth century. His wife, Margaret, was an invalid for most of her life. In 1875, she and Charles moved into the Parry Mansion, where her spinster sisters were able to help care for her.

Benjamin was known to have been public-spirited, scientific, and zealous for public improvements in the community. He was well read. A number of books including *Goldsmith's Animated Nature*, published in 1795, have been found in his home.

Later in his life, Benjamin wrote about his father in a letter to his wife, Jane:

> I have often thought of my father's advice to me about the time of my beginning in the business of the world, he advised me, "Think of the giver of the good things as well as the gift." I trust I will, not altogether unthoughtful though, fall short, perhaps of what I ought to have been.

At the dawn of the nineteenth century, Benjamin Parry was "king of the hill" in New Hope. He had expanded the mill industry in New Hope and owned a gristmill and sawmill on twenty-three acres of land that he had purchased across the Delaware River just south of Lambertville, New Jersey.[20] And he had invented a process that preserved grain for shipping to overseas markets. Parry was supervising the construction of the first bridge to New Jersey and was instrumental in establishing the town's first commercial bank. He was entertaining influential personalities in his elegant Georgian-style mansion in a town whose name had become widely identified with his resurrected New Hope Mills. He was a respected citizen, prominent entrepreneur, and loving husband and father who was deeply involved and very active in the development of his community.

At the same time, Benjamin Parry was a partner with James Cresson in the firm of Parry and Cresson, a flour commission and storage business located at 18 Strawberry Alley between Chestnut and Market (High) Streets in Old City Philadelphia.[21] The office was situated just one block from Christ Church, and the home of the treasurer of the United States, Alexander Hamilton, could be seen just over two blocks to the south. In the early years, Parry operated his businesses at other locations in the city, including Water Street and Vine Street near the Delaware River. Philadelphia was the capital of the United States with a population of about 41,000 people while Parry operated his businesses from 1790 to 1800. A Parry relative, Timothy Paxson, was also involved in the Philadelphia business. Later, Paxson was one of the executors of the estate of Stephen Girard.

In April 1806, Benjamin Parry hired Charles Pidcock of Bucks County to deliver his flour from New Hope to Philadelphia and to bring grain and flaxseed from Philadelphia to his mills in New Hope. There is an unconfirmed anecdote that indicates that at least one close encounter between Benjamin Parry and George Washington in Philadelphia may have occurred. Both Parry and Washington were involved in the flour business, and at one point, one of the hogsheads used for shipping the flour that belonged to Parry was erroneously attributed to Washington. Family records note that Benjamin Parry also owned a plantation in New London Township in Chester County, Pennsylvania.

Parry had become a successful businessman in a variety of enterprises and was greatly respected both in New Hope and in Philadelphia. But his greatest challenge lay ahead. William Maris had arrived in New Hope from Philadelphia in 1812 and soon became Parry's main competitor. In less than fifteen years, Maris had virtually surrounded the Parry dominion. He purchased more than two dozen parcels. Just two blocks west of Parry's home, Maris constructed the most formidable mills in the area. These Lepanto mills' twin towers could be seen from Parry's backyard. On the northeast section of town, Maris quickly constructed the Delaware House, one of the largest hotels in the area. On the north side just one block north of the Parry Mansion, Maris built a massive red brick residential building. And on the south end of town Maris was building the gigantic Union Paper Mills.

Then, for the coup de grâce, Maris built his mansion on a hill overlooking all of his and Parry's properties. "Cintra," as he called it, was a two-and-a-half-story fieldstone house with thick walls covered with yellow pebble dash that emulated a section of its counterpart—the palace in Cintra, Portugal, that had enchanted Maris on his visit there. The house was buttressed by two wings at its northeast and northwest levels. The rear elevation of this hub, in addition to the southeast and southwest elevations, is another full story above grade, creating perfect symmetry and proportion. This great residence is fan-shaped, similar to the Octagon House in Washington DC.

William Maris's "Cintra"
Courtesy of the New Hope Historical Society

Maris's rapid advances in developing his investments in the New Hope community undoubtedly rattled the normally unflappable Quaker persona of Benjamin Parry. His financial records show that he purchased ten acres of land adjacent to Maris's property, indicating the fierce competition that had developed between the town's two most prominent entrepreneurs. The training and advice that Benjamin had received from his father would soon be put to its greatest test. Disputes arose over the use of the Aquetong Creek. Parry owned the rights to the creek. The three million gallons of water carried by the creek through the area each day were vital to the operations of Parry's mill and to the other mill owners along the creek, including William Maris, who had built his own milldam just west of the Parry dam.

The stage was set for what was to become one of the most bitter and prolonged legal battles in the history of Bucks County, Pennsylvania: *Maris v. Parry.*

Maris v. Parry

Very little is known about the young, mysterious, and ambitious William Maris, who arrived in New Hope from Philadelphia after the War of 1812. He apparently enjoyed traveling abroad. The majestic home that he later built in New Hope was inspired by his travels in Portugal. After settling in New Hope, he began numerous ventures designing and constructing buildings and becoming involved with the newly established bridge company, even to the point of becoming its president. This applied more salt to the wounds that Benjamin had already experienced from the young up-start. Ironically, as we have seen, Parry's friend, Samuel Ingham, was the president of the bank that was licensed with the bridge company.

Over the years, because of freshets and floods, Parry was compelled to reconstruct the milldam near the Delaware River. Maris continually accused Parry of adversely affecting the operation of his mills along the Aquetong Creek by "willfully slowing up the flow of his water by raising the dam." This ongoing feud resulted in an extensive lawsuit that dragged on from 1821 to 1833. William Maris sued Parry for ten thousand dollars. Numerous depositions and testimonies for each side ensued. As the court fight continued over the years, Maris's unrelenting building frenzy began catching up with him, and he started losing properties to the sheriff.

Benjamin Parry patiently built his defense against the lawsuit that had been lodged against him. Records include certifications from engineers and witnesses who examined the milldam's dimensions on a number of occasions. His cousin, Jesse Betts, whom Parry had hired to build the dam, traveled to New Hope from Wilmington, Delaware, by stagecoach to testify. He left his sick bed, deeming it "his duty to attend ... since the case was such a notorious one."[22] In November 1828, engineers Charles Schlater and Joseph B. Conard certified in the presence of William Maris and Benjamin Parry that they had compared the levels of the milldam and found them to be correct.

The Mill Pond in New Hope
Photograph by Stephen T. Krencicki

Then in June 1832, a team of witnesses—including A. C. Brittain, Charles Ely, Oliver Parry, Richard Randolph, Merritt Reeder, Samuel Stockton, and Mordecai Thomas, all men of honor, distinction, and achievement in New Hope—testified that "all of the holes in the abutment correspond with each other and are on a true level with and same height [sic] at the top of the plate on the breast of said mill dam."[23] Parry was active in his own defense. Court records show that Parry cross-examined John Poor, a witness for Maris. Parry's thorough and incisive questioning forced Poor to admit that his testimony was "guesswork" and that he had, in fact, measured neither the height of the water in the dam nor the size of the water wheel. In 1833 the Doylestown Court of Common Pleas ruled in favor of Benjamin Parry.

William Maris failed in his efforts to take the case to a higher court. It was a disaster for him. Soon after, he lost the remainder of his properties, including his beloved "Cintra," which, as the fates would have it, was eventually purchased by Richard Randolph, a relative of Benjamin Parry. Maris set sail to Madeira, Spain, and then returned to Philadelphia, where he died just a few years later.

Benjamin Parry had won.

His mills and business ventures continued to be profitable until he retired and sold them just a couple of years later. While he was defending himself in the irksome and time-consuming litigation with Maris, Benjamin Parry faced more serious personal and business situations. His wife, Jane, while visiting relatives in Philadelphia in 1826, became seriously ill. Jane had been Benjamin's soul mate and confidante for nearly forty years. They traveled extensively together and spent many days in Philadelphia as Benjamin built his early flour exporting business there. On May 13, 1826, Jane Parry, the love of his life, died in Philadelphia.

Jane Paxson Parry, in whose childhood home in New Hope George Washington once slept, was laid to rest in the Friends Cemetery at Fourth and Arch Streets in Philadelphia near the final resting place of Benjamin Franklin in nearby Christ Church Cemetery.

In that same year, the bank that had been founded by Benjamin Parry and Samuel Ingham failed and was sold. Many years later, his grandson, Richard Randolph Parry, who was president of the bridge company in the beginning of the twentieth century, demonstrating the bitterness that still lingered with the Parrys about the Maris lawsuit, would write that "William Maris, the second president of the bank, wrecked and destroyed its business as is well known."[24] The resulting financial setback coupled with the recent death of his beloved wife must certainly have caused severe turmoil in Parry's life. At nearly seventy years of age, he had to face his life and his work without his closest and dearest friend. His wife had died, his bank had failed, and he was embroiled in an extended court case with his inveterate nemesis, William Maris.

But, with all of the problems plaguing Benjamin Parry in 1826, he was not distracted from the new developments that were taking place around the New Hope community. Plans were being formulated for the construction of the Delaware Canal, which would begin about thirty miles south of New Hope in Bristol, Pennsylvania. Soon the Irish and Polish immigrants were feverishly digging the new waterway toward New Hope. Local farmers and businessmen were signing up for their share in this new and promising business enterprise, and Benjamin Parry, who rarely shied away from entering any new business venture, was one of the first New Hope residents to invest in the construction of the new waterway that would, once again, put New Hope at the central point of the expanded commerce that was soon to come.

When completed, the Delaware Canal was connected to the Lehigh Canal to access the upstate Pennsylvania coal industry whose products it brought to Easton, Pennsylvania. This engineering marvel afforded safe and easy transportation from Easton to Bristol. There, the boats would be connected and towed down the Delaware River to Philadelphia and to the other towns along the river. Later, the canal boats would be linked to the markets in New York City. New Hope became the central point of the route between Easton and Bristol. New opportunities and employment brought greater prosperity to the town.

It was in New Hope where the canal boats, after 1840, switched to navigate across the Delaware River to the Delaware & Raritan Canal in Lambertville, New Jersey, and then make the long journey north toward New York City and Long Island. At its peak the canal brought nearly three thousand canal boats annually through New Hope with all of their commerce, trade, and workers with their families. Local commerce reaped rapid and substantial economic expansion from the new transportation system.

It is clear from his activities involving the construction of the Delaware Canal and his ongoing court case with William Maris that Benjamin Parry had remained active in his business and community affairs until he was well into his late seventies. Indeed, Parry's records reveal that in 1828, when he was seventy-one years old, he owned nearly one hundred acres in New Hope and twenty-three acres in New Jersey.[25]

Benjamin lived to see his nephew, John C. Parry, sworn in as the first burgess or mayor of New Hope when the borough was incorporated in 1837. John remained active in borough affairs for the remainder of his life providing continued support. After his one-year term as the first burgess, he was voted in to the borough council in 1838 and served several terms. He was the president of the council in 1860, the year of his death. Family correspondence shows that Benjamin's son, Oliver, was a major source of support for Benjamin and that Benjamin, in turn, had inspired the work ethic and character that were to prepare his son to become one of the major real estate developers in the city of Philadelphia in the middle of the nineteenth century.

On Friday, November 22, 1839, Benjamin Parry died in his beloved Parry Mansion. He had lived well into his eighty-second year. His passing was a monumental blow to the community that he had led for more than half a century. He was buried in the Solebury Friends cemetery and was remembered as follows:

> He was a member of the Society of Friends, and esteemed by a large circle of acquaintances as an honest and good citizen.
>
> *Bucks County Intelligencer*
> December 4, 1839

Benjamin Parry had fulfilled his father's advice. When young Benjamin began his business career, his father advised him to "think of the giver of good things as well as the gift." And he was true to the Parry family motto: "Learn to do right and God will protect you." He was a decent and honest man who left behind a lasting legacy for his family and his community.

CHAPTER 3
The Old York Road Connection

I f they had received frequent flyer-type bonus awards for travel on Old York Road in the eighteenth and nineteenth centuries, the Parry family undoubtedly would have been platinum-card holders. Benjamin and later his son, Oliver, traveled frequently and extensively on the major route connecting Philadelphia with Montgomery and Bucks Counties.

Historian W. W. H. Davis called it one of the five great highways of the county.[26] Old York Road is one of the oldest and most historic roadways in the United States. Its origin dates back thousands of years to the Native Americans who cut the original trails from Philadelphia to the Delaware River in Bucks County, Pennsylvania, where they fished, hunted, and grew crops. The Lenni-Lenape culture had been established there about five hundred years before William Penn arrived on the scene.

The road opened in 1711 as a rough-hewn route after rocks and trees were removed, bridges were built, and the road surface was covered with stones. In 1722, the right branch of the road opened from Willow Grove to Hatboro. Over the next few decades feeder roads were built to connect to the road, and they brought a dramatic increase of stage lines and freight. Commercial travel from communities along Old York Road to central New Jersey was booming. During the Revolutionary War, Old York Road was used almost exclusively for the transport of troops, material, and communications.

In the mid 1700s the first commercial means of travel began between Philadelphia, Montgomery, and Bucks Counties and New Hope. The Swift-Sure Stage Line offered passage each week in their initial years with a passenger fare equivalent to about five dollars. The coaches left the old Barley Sheaf tavern on Second Street near Race Street in Philadelphia,[27] just about three blocks from the later location of Benjamin Parry's flour exporting business on Strawberry Alley, at eight o'clock in the morning. They arrived in New Hope at the Ferry House Tavern, now the Logan Inn, just across the street from the present location of the Parry Mansion, about twelve hours later. The coaches stopped about every ten miles for refreshments for the weary travelers and to change the horses that pulled the coaches.

It was a long and brutal trip. Gaping holes and severe ruts in the road that were created by the removal of rocks and tree stumps were filled with dirt that was regularly washed out by rainwater. Parts of tree trunks were often laid over the open holes to allow passage, but it was brutally rough on the travelers. The twelve passengers who were normally carried on the coach were jostled around and clung to their seats anxiously anticipating the next stop for refreshments.

After the Revolutionary War, travel along Old York Road increased to a point where there was hardly a time of day that one would not see some type of transportation, be it Jersey wagons or Conestoga wagons or smaller vehicles. Major improvements were made in 1803 when the turnpike was authorized on the section from Rising Sun to the Red Lion Inn in Willow Grove, close to Benjamin Parry's boyhood home at the Manor of Moreland.[28] By 1827, the number of trips increased from one to three each week. The Swift-Sure Stage Line's already-burgeoning profits dramatically increased when it was awarded the mail contracts.

Benjamin Parry had a traveling desk manufactured for himself in Philadelphia around the year 1800 to meet his demands for maintaining his records and correspondence while traveling along Old York Road and elsewhere. The desk has a fold-over top that includes within it a series of compartments and beautiful green baize of finely woven wool. This baize acted as a cushion for the quill or pen, allowing the ink to flow smoothly. The compartment includes spaces for quills, an ink pot, pounce (a powdered drying agent), a shaker, writing paper, ledgers, and a drawer with an ingenious lock for documents. The desk enabled

Parry to travel with all of his required data at hand. The design and stable construction of the mahogany desk, which used a secondary wood of poplar, assured durability. It was an early-nineteenth-century equivalent to the ever-present laptop computers two centuries later. One can imagine Benjamin hard at work at his desk on the various coach stops along the road. Today, Parry's desk is displayed at the Parry Mansion.

Decades later when Oliver began his regular trips between Philadelphia and New Hope, life on the road became a lot more pleasant following many upgrades and road improvements that had been completed over the years. But family correspondence reveals that Oliver would ask his father to send a horse and carriage so that "Rachel and the children could travel to New Hope and the trip would be much more pleasanter than riding the stage, and we could save expense."

Old York Road became a legendary route because so many important events in American history occurred along its path. As the Parrys and other travelers journeyed north along Old York Road from Philadelphia in the late nineteenth and early twentieth centuries, they must surely have been delighted to view the sites of the many significant events that had occurred along the road that was a post road and main artery of travel between Philadelphia and New York City. Some of the original stones that were placed along the route before the Revolutionary War still existed along the south side of the road.

Passengers were refreshed and horses were changed at the Red Lion Inn in what is now Willow Grove. Joseph Butler built the inn in 1732. He was later captured by the British and taken to Philadelphia in 1777. Up to five stagecoach lines changed their horses at the inn before the Civil War. It is said that about three hundred horses could be kept overnight at the location. The inn could provide sleeping accommodations for about one hundred men who would sleep on blankets placed on the floor of the tavern.[29] The inn was destroyed by fire in 1880 and, since 1868, no longer served the traveling public as an inn. The Willow Inn now occupies the site of this most historically important tavern.

The Willow Inn
Photograph by Stephen T. Krencicki

From Willow Grove the route led to Hatboro, where a memorial celebrates the spirited Battle of Crooked Billet between the British soldiers and the Continental Army. Then, in Warminster, the road passes near the home of John Fitch, the inventor of the first boat to be powered by steam.

Just a few miles east of Warminster, near Hartsville, travelers could see the tiny (about twenty feet wide by twenty feet long) "Log College" that was founded in 1726. Just twenty years later in Elizabeth, New Jersey, it played a major role in the founding of the College of New Jersey, now Princeton University.[30] The college was the first American Presbyterian theological seminary. It is considered to be the predecessor of Princeton University, because several of its teachers and graduates served in important posts at Princeton before and after the university was founded in 1746. About six months after it was founded, five graduates of the Log College—Samuel Blair, Gilbert Tennent, William Tennent Jr., Samuel Finley, and Richard Treat—were elected trustees of Princeton University. Mr. Finley eventually became the fifth president of the university.

The Log College Memorial
Photograph by Stephen T. Krencicki

Right after crossing the Neshaminy Creek, travelers passed near the Moland House, General George Washington's headquarters at Neshaminy Camp. There Washington's Continental Army of 11,000 troops camped for nearly two weeks—the longest encampment of the army in any Pennsylvania town. It was there that the French General Lafayette reported for duty. It is astounding to imagine the long encampment of thousands of soldiers on both sides of this legendary road for many miles.

As Old York Road climbed east to Furlong, travelers were greeted by the majestic sight of Buckingham Mountain, the second highest point in Bucks County at 750 feet. Then about two and a half miles east, in Buckingham, the General Greene Inn is reached at the corner of Durham Road. The stately colonial building had been a roadside tavern for travelers for more than a century and a half. Originally known as Bogart's Tavern, it was licensed in 1763. It was the headquarters of the Committee of Observation and Inspection, which first organized the revolutionary movement in Bucks County in 1775 and 1776.

This was where the county's first military organizations of the revolution mustered in 1775. Here it was that in 1776, General Nathaniel

Greene issued the order to the troops to gather the Durham boats for General George Washington's epic crossing of the Delaware River for the surprise attack on the Hessians at Trenton that helped turn the course of the war. George Washington ordered General Charles Lee to Coryell's Ferry in June 1778, and Washington and Lafayette were to follow. However, the stubborn Old York Road refused to let them pass because heavy rains had mired it in mud, making it impossible to move the heavy artillery over the frequently difficult road. Alas, General Washington and his troops were forced to spend the night in beautiful Buckingham.

Bogart's Tavern
Photograph by Stephen T. Krencicki

Buckingham Mountain was a station on the Underground Railroad, sheltering slaves traveling north before the Civil War. Then in Holicong (Buckingham Valley), travelers passed through the place where in 1775 Isaac Still, an Indian and leader of the tribe, is said to have led the last forty or so of the Lenni-Lenape Indians out of the Delaware Valley on the long trek westward.

Just about one mile east, travelers passed the grand Elm Grove, home of the prominent Colonel and Mrs. Henry D. Paxson. He was a member of the Philadelphia and Bucks County Bar Associations, a prominent Philadelphia lawyer, and an avid student of history. Colonel Paxson had a number of residences in Philadelphia in the 1890s, the last of which was located at 1409 Locust Street, just about three blocks from the future residence of Oliver Randolph Parry at 1604 Pine Street. The Bucks County home of Colonel Paxson and his wife, Hannameel Canby, was known as Elm Grove, a fifty-acre farm in Holicong. His son, Henry Douglas Paxson, was a lawyer with the prestigious Philadelphia firm of Dilworth and Paxson. Their daughter-in-law, Adele Corning Warden Paxson, was an ardent supporter of opera and vocal arts in the city of Philadelphia.

Elm Grove
Photograph by Stephen T. Krencicki

Then, Benjamin Parry must have frequently felt a touch of nostalgia as the coach traveled up the hill heading east from Elm Grove. There the stately Buckingham Friends Meeting House graced the crest of a hill on the north side, as it still does today. The meetinghouse was built in 1768, replacing the old house that had burned down in the previous year. It had been used as a hospital for the troops during the Revolutionary War, and some of those who died there are buried in the cemetery on the grounds. Benjamin Parry changed his meeting membership to

Buckingham from his family's meetinghouse in Horsham in 1785. In that year he took over the operations of the mills in New Hope from the Todd family. Buckingham was the closest meetinghouse to New Hope, then Coryell's Ferry, at that time. The Solebury Friends Meeting House had not been opened until 1806. It was at the Buckingham Friends Meeting House that Benjamin Parry had married Jane Paxson on November 14, 1787. No doubt the memories of their wedding rushed back to Benjamin and Jane as they so often rode by the beautiful Georgian stone structure that had been constructed by the master builder, Mathias Hutchison.[31]

Two final stops were needed along the route to reach New Hope. The last five miles on Old York Road between the Buckingham Friends Meeting House and New Hope ran along the Lahaska–New Hope Turnpike. Travelers were required to pull up to the first toll gatekeeper's house that was located on the southwest corner of Aquetong Road and Old York Road. The first tolls were collected on the turnpike in 1852. The toll for a horse and rider was five cents, and a coach and four horses netted a fee of twenty-five cents. One could even get a speeding ticket and fine of twenty dollars for driving faster than eight miles an hour.

Finally, it was on to New Hope. The road passed the estate of Benjamin Parry's great friend and partner, Samuel D. Ingham, and the beautiful, sparkling Ingham Spring (formerly the Aquetong Spring) that feeds the Ingham Creek (formerly the Aquetong Creek) flowing two miles east to New Hope. Both bodies of water were renamed in honor of Samuel D. Ingham. The spring is considered one of the natural wonders of southeastern Pennsylvania. This is the waterway that powered the numerous mills that sprang up along its banks and helped to make New Hope the great industrial and manufacturing town in the eighteenth and nineteenth centuries.

Buckingham Friends Meeting House
Photograph by Stephen T. Krencicki

Just about a mile east of the Ingham House, the final toll gatekeeper located on the corner of Sugan Road and Old York Road collected his fees. After that brief stop, the worn and weary travelers, having been tossed about on the full day's journey from Philadelphia, finally arrived in the welcoming town of New Hope, where travelers have discovered rest and relaxation for nearly three hundred years. Today, however, in place of the old Ferry House's frugal morsels and bare-bones accommodations, the Logan Inn provides travelers with dining of the finest cuisine and overnight relaxation in one of the most comfortable inns in Bucks County. And travelers can dine at dozens of restaurants, browse in unique shops, and enjoy a show at the Bucks County Playhouse, the state theater that now encompasses Benjamin Parry's eighteenth-century gristmill.

The Samuel D. Ingham House
Photograph by Stephen T. Krencicki

Ingham Spring
Photograph by Stephen T. Krencicki

Oliver Parry
Courtesy of the New Hope Historical Society

CHAPTER 4
Oliver Parry—Pioneer of Philadelphia's Spring Garden Neighborhood

$$\approx$$

Benjamin Parry's only son, Oliver, was born on December 20, 1794, during his father's rise to prominence in New Hope. By the time Oliver was twenty years old, his father had successfully promoted and supervised the construction of the bridge from New Hope, Pennsylvania, to Lambertville, New Jersey, and the bridge company had taken control of most of the shipping across the river. Benjamin had previously purchased the ferry operations and shut them down when the bridge that he was the first to support financially opened in 1813. Benjamin's patented invention for grain preservation was gaining popularity around the country. Oliver learned firsthand from his father about the complexities of the business world and, as current entrepreneurs would say, the art of the deal.

Oliver Parry married Rachel Randolph in Philadelphia on May 1, 1827, and he appears to have spent most of his adult life there, eventually calling the Parry Mansion in New Hope his "summer home." His wife, Rachel, and her family were originally from Perth Amboy, New Jersey, and were steeped in patriotism. They were the most prolific and one of the most influential early Quaker families that settled in New Jersey. Her mother was Anna Julianna Steel. Her father, Major Edward Fitz Randolph, was a printer who was apprenticed to a printer named

Parker in New York City. Parker was a close friend of the preeminent Philadelphian, Benjamin Franklin.

Randolph was prominent in the Revolutionary War, taking part in the Battles of Trenton, Princeton, Brandywine, Germantown, and Monmouth. He also fought in the Valley Forge campaign. He belonged to the brigade commanded by General Anthony Wayne and commanded the outlying guard consisting of a sergeant, corporal, and sixteen privates of the 4th Pennsylvania Regiment at the Battle of Paoli, where they faced a British advance guard of dragoons, riflemen, and light infantry, a total of about fifty men. Major Randolph was severely wounded, losing the sight in one of his eyes, and half of his men were killed or wounded. In a love letter written to his then fiancée, Anna Julianna Steel, Major Randolph echoed the lament of so many valiant soldiers when he wrote:

> The thoughts of being at so great distance from you, without being able to see you, before I depart, the least probability of my hearing from you. After I am gone and until I return—make me unhappy, past description. The danger I have to pass through does not in the least trouble me—though it must be confessed—it is very vexatious— after having undergone every fatigue, hardship and danger, in fighting of the Inglish [sic] in this Quarter.... But I shall dwell no longer on a subject which I imagine to be disagreeable to you—but recommend you to the care and protection, of an all sufficient God. And until I shall be so happy as to see you again, believe me to be, with the greatest respect and esteem—Your unhappy—tho constant lover.
>
> Edward F. Randolph
> July 21, 1778[32]

After the war, Major Parry returned to Philadelphia where, in a few years, he became one of the largest East India merchants in the city. He died in 1837 in his eighty-fourth year. Rachel was a lineal descendent of Governor Waldron, a colonial governor of New Hampshire. It was

Rachel's brother, Richard Randolph, who purchased "Cintra," the home of William Maris, the former major competitor of the Parry family, in 1830, after Maris went bankrupt and left New Hope. How happy Randolph must have made his new in-laws just three years after Oliver and Rachel wed.

Oliver and Rachel had twelve children, all of whom were born in the Parry Mansion in New Hope. Eight of the children survived to adulthood, and Oliver's father, Benjamin, lived to enjoy seeing four of his grandchildren padding around the old Parry Mansion. Oliver's fourth son, Edward Randolph Parry, like his grandfather and namesake, distinguished himself in the United States Army. He served as a first lieutenant of the 11th Infantry beginning in 1861, and he served until the end of the Civil War. He was adjutant general of the regular brigade, became captain in 1864, and later became major for "gallant and meritorious service." Major Edward Randolph Parry was present at army headquarters in 1865 when Robert E. Lee surrendered. Edward Randolph Parry died in 1871 from wounds that he had suffered in the Civil War.

Edward and Richard earlier had become prominent in the financial field and established a bank in Mankato, Minnesota, where they had completed their education. Mankato maintains a gruesome historical significance. The land on which it is located was purchased by the United States government under a treaty with the Dakota Indians in 1851. The federal government's failure to make several payments to the Dakota nation led to the United States–Dakota conflict in 1862.

In a letter to Richard and Edward Parry, their uncle, Richard Randolph, alluded to the problems that had been occurring prior to the conflict and demonstrated the strong feelings that existed at the time:

> If I was out there I should certainly sigh for fine Chincoteague or Egg Harbor oysters.... As you don't mention anything about venison, or prairie fowls or such like ... I suppose the Indians have devoured them all long ago. Take care they don't devour you too. That country belongs to them by right and by inheritance, and everything in it is theirs', fish, flesh and fowl.

Uncle Richard goes on to chide his nephews about their prosperity: "As you appear to have grown so corpulent and fat, your carcasses will furnish many a dainty piece for their bacchanalian feasts."

After the Dakota Conflict, the United States Army perpetrated one of the largest mass executions in US history there. Thirty-eight Dakota Indians were brutally hanged for their involvement in the conflict. President Abraham Lincoln prevented an even more enormous tragedy when he pardoned 265 Native Americans, claiming that they had legitimately defended themselves against the US forces. The city's population was less than five thousand people when the Parrys operated their bank there in the 1860s. Later it became a railroad hub for the Midwest. The Parry brothers had been among the initial investors and brokers in the plan for the development of the rail transportation system in that area. Today, Mankato boasts nearly 37,000 residents and is the county seat of Blue Earth County, Minnesota.

Oliver and Rachel Parry's daughter Mary Randolph Parry married Dr. Joseph Gibbons Richardson on January 6, 1864. Dr. Richardson was an eminent physician in Philadelphia, specializing in microscopic research, blood analysis, and hygiene.

Oliver Parry came of age as his father was experiencing what was most certainly the most difficult and trying years of his life. Just one year before Oliver married Rachel, his mother, Jane, died and his father was deep into the long court battle with William Maris. Parry family records show that Oliver was his father's bedrock during those troublesome years. As early as three years before Benjamin died, Oliver took responsibility for the family's business affairs. In 1836, Oliver negotiated an agreement for the rental of the gristmill and a small frame house in the vicinity for a rental price of eight hundred dollars per year that included the provision that the renter would be responsible to pay the taxes and repairs. He also took the lead in negotiating rental agreements for some of the Parrys' farmland in the area.

Oliver Parry Takes the Reins

Following Benjamin's death in 1839, Oliver Parry, who had inherited a portion of his father's property, acquired most of the remaining property from his sisters, Ruth and Jane. Only a small part of Benjamin Parry's property remained in the hands of his ailing sister Margaret, wife of

Charles Knowles. Later, Oliver sold property that was located just west of the Parry Mansion on Ferry Street.

Although Oliver Parry had begun to focus his attention on his real estate investments in Philadelphia before 1830, he continued to conduct business in New Hope for the property that he later inherited from his father. Less than a month after the disastrous flood of February 7, 1841, Oliver rented the Parry water gristmill and the Parry Mansion to Morris Matthews and Hiram Ely for eight hundred dollars for one year. The lease included rights to the water and machinery for the mill. Matthews and Ely were responsible for all taxes for the year, and Parry reserved the right to use any surplus water at the location. In 1865, Oliver and his wife, Rachel, and his sisters along with his brother-in-law, Charles Knowles (Oliver's sister, Margaret, had continued to suffer from her lifelong illness), sold most of the remaining part of the original sixteen acres that their father, Benjamin, had purchased as a young man in 1785.

The family maintained possession of the legendary Parry Mansion, which continued to be the Parry family's residence for more than a hundred years longer until 1966. An interesting tax receipt in the family records shows that Oliver paid $16.80 for school taxes in New Hope for the full year of 1872. Oliver and Rachel spent most of their time at their residence in Philadelphia, using the Parry Mansion as a peaceful weekend and summer retreat away from the bustling city. Their correspondence also reveals that the Parry family was fond of visiting Cape May, New Jersey, for summer relaxation at the popular New Jersey shore resort.

Oliver Parry continued to possess rights to the Delaware River that his father had secured for control of the river for one mile north and one mile south of the ferry landing. In 1870, Parry granted fishery rights to Hiram Scarborough for a payment of rent that was specified as "thirty-two shad or their average value in cash to be paid on the first day of July of each year." It also required that Scarborough pay all taxes that may be assessed on the property. Scarborough went on to operate a shad fishery. For many years it was a local tradition that the first shad that was caught each year was presented to the Parry family. At its peak in 1896, shad fisheries along the Delaware River and Delaware Bay netted about nineteen million pounds of shad. Fish caught in the

New Hope area were packed in ice and shipped to New York City and Philadelphia markets. In that same year Parry leased the Parry family's barn, reserving rights for his private storage.

Numerous family records demonstrate Oliver Parry's business acumen. A vivid example is seen in a transaction that was recorded in 1853. In that year Parry leased nine lots on Chatham Street in Philadelphia to Meyers Hudson and Robert Hudson for a total annual rent of $414 on which to build three-story brick dwelling houses equal in value to the homes erected by noted builder Josiah Haines, who was constructing homes in the neighborhood at the time. The lease required that Parry and Randolph supply the bricks and lumber for the construction. After collecting about $4,200 in rental fees over the ten-year period, Parry took the lots back for $200.

Oliver and his nephew, Nathaniel Randolph, formed a partnership for what would eventually become one of the most extensive real estate developments in Philadelphia in the middle of the nineteenth century. Nathaniel was the son of Edward Randolph, Rachel's brother. Records indicate that Oliver and Nathaniel had insured a row house that was located at 1301 Spruce Street, the northwest corner, as early as December 1844.[33] Nathaniel Randolph married Phebe Hunter Sinton on June 1, 1845. Parry and Randolph began their venture by purchasing land on the northeast and southeast corners of Monroe and Hancock Streets in 1848, and in the following year they bought property on the southwest corner of Front and Birch Streets in the district of Kensington.

The Bush Hill Estates
Courtesy of the John Carter Brown Library

Oliver's Philadelphia residence was located at 1721 Arch Street from 1861 until his death in 1874[34] on part of the property that now includes the Verizon building, one of the tallest high-rise buildings in the city of Philadelphia, directly across the street from the location of the manse for the Arch Street Presbyterian Church. It was also under construction at the time when Parry was beginning his development of the Spring Garden area in 1853, and it was completed in 1855. The church is now included on the National Register of Historic Places. In January 2007, Charles, Prince of Wales, and his wife, Camilla, Duchess of Cornwall, attended services at the church less than fifty feet from the site of Oliver Parry's residence when they visited Philadelphia. In 1969, Charles was crowned Prince of Wales at Caernarfon Castle in Caernarvonshire, Wales, the birthplace of Oliver Parry's ancestors.

1700 Block of Arch Street in 1913
Courtesy of the City of Philadelphia, Department of Records

Philadelphia in the Mid-Nineteenth Century

Philadelphia in the middle of the nineteenth century was struggling to gain its momentum after the tumultuous years of the Industrial Revolution. Roving gangs of marauders and the absence of any viable law enforcement presented untold challenges to residents and visitors alike. The city was growing way beyond its original Revolutionary War footprint. Slums developed around the city, and thousands of its residents lived in filth, infestation, and squalor. As the city's population grew dramatically during that time, there was an even greater need for decent and safe housing. The extensive poverty of its citizens left Philadelphia with an urgent need to promote the growth of affordable dwellings. The police and fire departments were reformed and expanded. And the city took stock of its water supply and acted to rebuild and improve its systems. The Spring Garden water system was one of the first to be addressed.

Parry and Randolph concentrated their real estate development efforts on the historic Bush Hill Estates area in what is now the historic Spring Garden District of Philadelphia. Bush Hill, more than 150 acres, was originally in 1740 the estate of Andrew Hamilton, attorney for William Penn. He was probably the first "Philadelphia lawyer" because of his shrewd representation of William Penn and his sons in their numerous land pursuits. Hamilton was the designer of Independence Hall. Unfortunately, for Hamilton, he died just one year after his manor was completed. Bush Hill was also, for a time, the home of the vice president of the United States, John Adams. The country home was located in the area that is now Buttonwood Street between Seventeenth and Eighteenth Streets.

Strolling through the shaded and peaceful streets in the Spring Garden section of the city today, it is hard to imagine the sordid history of the place. When yellow fever began claiming thousands of lives in the 1790s, it was becoming impossible to address the issues that its victims had presented. Dr. Benjamin Rush, physician and signer of the Declaration of Independence, had diagnosed the disease. It was then believed that yellow fever was carried to the city from what is now Haiti in the wet spring of 1793 by an infected refugee. The symptoms of the fever included nausea, skin eruptions, black vomit, incontinence, jaundice, and, in numerous cases, death. Fearing the spread of the virus, the city's hospital and almshouse refused to admit yellow fever victims.

The old Andrew Hamilton estate at Bush Hill had been experiencing steady decline since its sale in 1814. Hamilton's Bush Hill home was located on the hill just behind what is now the Free Library of Philadelphia. It had deteriorated miserably over the years. Patients had at first been moved to the "outskirts" of the city at Twelfth and Market (then High) Streets. But, when even that location became untenable, the decision was made to move the masses of yellow fever victims to the Bush Hill Estates property.

It was there that the city decided to send the victims of the yellow fever epidemic. Bush Hill, once the grand residence of Pennsylvania's greatest lawyer and confidante of William Penn, became the depository of the sick and dying. By the end of 1793, when the epidemic finally had relented, it is estimated that about five thousand Philadelphians had died. That was more than ten percent of the city's population. Half of the population of the city had fled, and government ground to a halt. Richard G. Miller in the book *Philadelphia: A 300-Year History* reported that the federal capital had become a ghost city.[35]

Bush Hill Estates

George Washington placed a local grocer, Stephen Girard, in charge of the administration of the nearly impossible situation. Girard took full control of Bush Hill and turned it into a functioning hospital. His reputation for the effective management and resolution of the Bush Hill nightmare was widespread as a result of this amazing success. It was the beginning of his legendary career in finance. The former sea captain, ship owner, and grocer founded and was sole owner of the Girard Bank that flourished in Philadelphia until nearly the end of the twentieth century.

Stephen Girard's will financed the construction and endowment of Girard College. Located near the old Bush Hill Estates area, the college was originally established to provide education for poor, white, fatherless boys, but in the twentieth century the school opened its doors to girls and boys of all races. Girard College's curriculum has evolved with the changing times as well.[36] Originally the school prepared students for trades, professions, and apprenticeship training. Today Girard prepares its students for college and technological careers. The death of a father is no longer a requirement for admission. Stephen Girard's will provided what is considered to have been the largest private charitable donation in American history at that time. Timothy Paxson, who was a business partner of Benjamin Parry, later was selected to be one of the executors of the will of Stephen Girard.

1700 Block of Arch Street in 2010

Later, in 1809, the site of Hamilton's mansion became the location of the Bush Hill Iron Works. It was established by Oliver Evans. His company enjoyed a popular reputation for its quality of manufacturing sugar, sawmill, and gristmill machinery at that location.

Philadelphia's Act of Consolidation in 1854 was essentially created to help govern the continuing growth of its population and industry beginning with an attempt to establish law and order. Speculative housing and development were also spurred by the act. The legislation provided that the city should be enlarged by including all of the territory that was located within the county of Philadelphia. The incorporated districts were dissolved. The city was divided into twenty-four wards.

The thirteenth, fourteenth, and fifteen wards included nearly the entire Spring Garden District. The Baldwin Locomotive Works located nearby was the nation's largest builder of locomotive engines and was a major factor in the development of the neighborhood. Around 1809 the Bush Hill Iron Works was located almost on the exact site of Andrew Hamilton's home. Other heavy industries producing mill machinery and steam engines were also located there around that time.

The Philadelphia and Columbia Railroad, later known as the Philadelphia and Reading Railroad, which began operating in the area in the 1830s, delivered raw materials, like coal, to the local industries and carried out their finished products to the rest of the country. The tracks of the railroad ran along Pennsylvania Avenue, directly through the heart of the Spring Garden District, along part of the old Delaware and Schuylkill Canal bed, which was never completed. So there was a great and growing need for housing for the thousands of employees whose ranks were steadily increasing in the district.

The Philadelphia Historical Commission has noted that "business partners Oliver Parry and Nathaniel Randolph constructed at least three hundred speculative row houses throughout the Spring Garden Historic District." The commission noted that these were "spacious row and semi-detached houses, wide sidewalks and generous street widths of the Spring Garden Historic District ... [that] ... all emphasized relief from the congestion of the Old City and Society Hill. The latest comforts in plumbing, central heating and lighting were now affordable, and these attracted new middle income residents." The commission offers the following description of the new neighborhood:

Most of the new houses were built in the Italianate style. They had smooth brick fronts, large bracketed cornices and ornamental entrances. The significant group of "terrace" houses on the south side of Green Street between 15th and 17th Streets were the first speculative dwellings built in the Spring Garden neighborhood. Appealing to the middle class citizens who were attracted to this area, the notable feature of these houses was a small grass plot, often raised or terraced, in front of each dwelling. The green space suggested the escape from the congestion of the City, in addition to being an emblem of status.

Philadelphia Historic Commission
The Spring Garden Historic District
A Guide for Property Owners

Oliver Parry and Nathaniel Randolph were among the first builders of speculative housing in the neighborhood. Before their involvement, there was little development in the area. It was rather far removed from Philadelphia's business district, and there was no reliable and affordable transportation to the neighborhood. It had been mostly farmland that had been divided between the Andrew Hamilton and Robert Morris families, each of whom maintained large "country" residences there. The original name of Spring Garden Street was Morris Street.

When the Spring Garden District was consolidated in 1854, it encompassed about 1,100 acres. This was an area just slightly larger than the entire size of the New Hope, Pennsylvania, community in which Oliver Parry had been born.

Parry and Randolph began purchasing property in the Bush Hill Estates before 1830. In 1851, they bought land on the south side of Pratt Street and on the north side of what is now Fairmount Avenue near Nixon Street. In January 1853, they bought land on the south side of Green Street and the east side of Seventeenth and Eighteenth Streets, and on the north side of Green Street and the west side of Seventeenth Street. They continued their investments by buying two parcels of land on the west side of Sixteenth Street to Washington Street and leased each for $630 per year and purchased two parcels on the west side of Seventeenth Street to Washington Street, which they also leased for $630.50 per year. These transactions were followed by their purchase of two smaller parcels, one on the north side and one on the south side of Seventeenth Street to Centre Street, each of which they leased for a sum of ninety dollars per year.[37]

1500 Green Street
Photograph by Stephen T. Krencicki

1500 Block of Green Street
Photograph by Stephen T. Krencicki

1709–1713 Green Street
Photograph by Stephen T. Krencicki

2112–2114 Green Street
Photograph by Stephen T. Krencicki

2144–2146 Green Street
Photograph by Stephen T. Krencicki

Morning Light Interior, Daniel Garber, American, 1880–1958
Oil on Canvas, 1923
Philadelphia Museum of Art, Gift of Elise Robinson
From the Sallie Crozer Hilprecht Collection, 1945

Parry and Randolph's investments grew extensively as they continued to purchase land in the Spring Garden District from February to May 1853. In February, they extended their purchases to Nineteenth Street on the south side of Green Street to Centre Street. It is an interesting coincidence that the great New Hope Impressionist painter, Daniel Garber, would reside on this block seventy years later with his family.

Garber, whose main residence was located just about four miles north of New Hope, divided his time between the two residences while teaching at the Pennsylvania Academy of the Fine Arts for nearly forty years. His famous painting *Morning Light, Interior* was completed in 1923. It depicted his eldest daughter, Tanis, standing by the window in the living room of the townhouse that had been located at 1819 Green Street. The painting is now the property of the Philadelphia Museum of Art but is not currently on display there. Garber would use the room in at least two other paintings, including *South Room— Green Street* (1921), now at the Corcoran Gallery in Washington DC, and *Interior, Green Street* (1923), now the property of the Muskegon Museum of Art in Michigan. The living room of the home faced south and was drenched in sunlight during the day with the sun serving as the principal subject of the paintings. Unfortunately, the residence has long since been paved over, succumbing to the need for a parking lot at a neighborhood school.

In May 1853, Parry and Randolph continued their purchase of land in the Spring Garden District with the acquisition of the north side of Centre Street and the west side of Fifteenth Street. It appears that Oliver's son Edward Randolph Parry had joined his father in investing in the development of Green Street. Records indicate that Edward helped to finance the construction of homes from 2100 to 2118 Green Street.[38] Then, in November 1855, they bought the entire block of Mount Vernon Street between Twenty-First and Twenty-Second Streets for a total of $41,000. Later, in 1858, they sold sixteen houses from 1606 to 1618 Mount Vernon Street to Robert Paschall for $36,400.

The Parry and Randolph homes were mostly the Italianate style that typically featured a rusticated basement and embellished window and door surrounds. Other features included double-leaf doors, elaborate bracketed cornices, and arched and rounded forms. Red brick and marble were the major materials that they used in the construction.

Crisp, white marble entrances and marble lintels, sills, and steps graced the front of the homes. The availability of mass-produced ironwork for railings, fences, and gates through local manufacturers stimulated their extensive use by Parry and the other developers in the Spring Garden District.

Machine-carved marble and woodwork produced locally greatly enhanced the building facades, and these beautiful ornamental features continue to grace the homes in Spring Garden to this day. Most of the buildings were three stories in height, but a number of them were four stories. Parry and Randolph sold some of the parcels to other local developers who brought their individual architectural styles to the neighborhood. The variety of architectural designs is most prominent on Green Street and Mount Vernon Street, where the north and south sides of the streets exhibit a wonderful array of architectural styles.

Oliver Parry's father, Benjamin, had obtained a sizable portion of land along the Lehigh River near Easton, Pennsylvania, which was used to supply the lumber for his mill in New Hope. Vast numbers of trees from that area and more of them to the north were harvested and shipped down the Delaware River and later by way of the Delaware Canal to New Hope for the lumber mills. Numerous houses and buildings in the growing city of Philadelphia were constructed with lumber from that area.

Oliver expanded his father's lumber business. He and his business partner, Nathaniel Randolph, continued to be listed in city directories as "lumber merchants." The Philadelphia City Directory shows that Nathaniel lived at 701 Green Street in 1856 and at 1709 Green Street in 1858. In addition to supplying lumber for their own housing development in the Spring Garden District, they had also provided the lumber for other developers. Records indicate that Oliver Parry's son, Richard Randolph Parry, had also been a lumber merchant at that time, most probably working with his father.

The Parry and Randolph lumberyards in Philadelphia were located at Broad Street, north of Green Street, and on Seventeenth and Green Streets. It was a bustling area of manufacturing and industry. The mammoth Baldwin Locomotive Works was located just two blocks south of the Parry and Randolph lumberyards. They also operated a lumberyard at Broad and Washington Streets in the city. Edward

Randolph Parry had assisted them with the business and lived with Oliver and Rachel at 633 Arch Street at that time. The Parry family also continued their involvement with Parry, Custis, and Company of Philadelphia. Blue jeans seem to have been the most popular sales item. As late as 1872, two years before Oliver Parry's death, the company had purchased thousands of yards of cadet-blue Marengo from West End Mills. Records indicate that the company manufactured and sold clothing in large quantities until it was dissolved in 1873.

The Hoopes and Townsend Company manufactured nuts, bolts, and rivets in its plant on Buttonwood Street, and the machine shops of Bancroft and Seller (later known as William Sellers and Company) lined Pennsylvania Avenue between Sixteenth and Seventeenth Streets, just two blocks south of the Parry and Randolph housing developments. Farther south on Callowhill Street, the Pennsylvania Soap Works provided hundreds of jobs, as it became the largest manufacturer of soap in Pennsylvania by 1880.

But Baldwin Locomotive Works dominated the area and soon became the most successful builder of locomotives in the world. Matthias Baldwin was a jeweler and machinist who built a steam engine for his business before 1830. Shortly after that time, the Philadelphia Museum commissioned Baldwin to build a miniature locomotive to help demonstrate the new technology. The demonstration was so effective that it brought the first order for a full-size locomotive from the Philadelphia, Germantown, and Norristown Railroad Company. Baldwin completed the job about a year later and his company was on its way to becoming the largest of its kind in the world. He continued to expand his business farther west from Hamilton and Spring Garden Streets from Broad Street all the way to Eighteenth Street, about four blocks. At its peak, Baldwin Locomotive Works employed 19,000 workers who labored on day and night shifts to supply the worldwide demand for the Baldwin locomotives. The plant covered more than sixteen acres in the rapidly growing western part of the city.

BROAD STREET FRONT OF BALDWIN LOCOMOTIVE WORKS.

The Baldwin Locomotive Works
Courtesy of the City of Philadelphia, Department of Records

Coincidentally, one of Matthias Baldwin's major partners and the superintendent of the massive company was Charles T. Parry. There is no indication, however, that he was directly related to Oliver Parry, whose company was building hundreds of homes near the sprawling locomotive works on Broad and Spring Garden Streets. Baldwin's company continued to grow despite the declining industry, and his success was attributed to his conservative business methods, sound engineering, and basic good management. In 1912, Baldwin Locomotive Works outgrew the land it needed in its original location just outside the Spring Garden District. It moved its operations to Eddystone, Pennsylvania, in 1912, where it continued to expand to cover 564 acres and at its peak produced about 30 locomotives per day. It was the largest employer in Philadelphia before World War I and manufactured artillery shells and gun mounts for the war effort. Parry's grandson, Oliver Randolph Parry, later became one of nearly 60,000 Philadelphians who would serve in that war.

By the time Baldwin Locomotive Works ceased production and

closed its doors in 1956, it had built more than 76,000 locomotives for companies around the world. The old Baldwin plants in Philadelphia were torn down in 1937, and the Boeing Company now occupies most of the site to which Baldwin had relocated in Eddystone. It is fascinating to note that one of the original Baldwin locomotives, the "Old Number 40," has been preserved by the New Hope & Ivyland Railroad and is still in use today in New Hope. The original railroad station was saved and preserved by the New Hope Historical Society, whose headquarters are located in the Parry Mansion in New Hope, the former home of Benjamin and Oliver Parry. A magnificent bronze sculpture of Matthias Baldwin stands on the north side of Philadelphia's city hall facing directly north to the former location of Baldwin Locomotive Works, less than a mile north on Broad Street at Spring Garden Street.

Philadelphia was turning the corner and rapidly becoming the first great American city. Within sight of the Parry and Randolph real estate development and Baldwin Locomotive Works, the Philadelphia Catholic Cathedral of Saints Peter and Paul was under construction on Eighteenth Street on what is now the Benjamin Franklin Parkway. By 1850, the side walls of the cathedral were already being constructed and towered forty-five feet over Eighteenth Street. A few blocks south, the grand Philadelphia Academy of Music was rising on South Broad Street and opened its doors for its first concert in January 1857.

Oliver Parry was a friend of Richard Vaux, the mayor of the city of Philadelphia at the time. Family records reveal that Oliver and the mayor vacationed together on at least one occasion at Heath House on Schooley's Mountain, a New Jersey retreat that advertised "Pure Mountain Air, No Hay Fever, No Mosquitoes and No Malaria."[39] Although Vaux failed to win reelection to the mayoral office in 1858, he continued to be quite active in the Democratic Party and was very influential in politics for the remainder of his life. Richard Vaux also followed his father's lead in helping to reform the penal system and became one of the country's experts in penology. He did much of his work with the Eastern State Penitentiary, which is located on what is now Fairmount Avenue, just about two blocks north of Oliver Parry's properties in the Spring Garden neighborhood.

In the following year, horse-drawn carriages started to provide transportation to North Philadelphia and back. East-west routes traveled along Green Street between Broad and Twenty-Second Streets. In 1859, the new Green and Coates Street Railway stable opened just outside the Spring Garden District at the corner of what is now Twenty-Fourth Street and Fairmount Avenue. The renowned architect, Theophilus Parsons Chandler Jr.—noted for his grand ecclesiastical style and designer of such great homes as "Pohego" for Judge James A. Logan in Bala and "Fox Hill," the home of Rudulphus Ellis, in Haverford—were lured to Philadelphia by the famous landscape artist, Robert Copeland. Chandler began to construct homes on properties adjacent to those being developed by Parry and Randolph. A beautiful example of Chandler's style can be seen in the mansion that he had built for Philadelphia industrialist Cyrus Cadwallader, which is located at 2018 Green Street.

The Victorian-style home featuring a marble vestibule with Pennsylvania walnut mantle and stained-glass transoms clearly shows how the development of the Spring Garden District was becoming grander as the years progressed. The Philadelphia Historical Commission reports that during the last quarter of the nineteenth century, the Spring Garden neighborhood had become home to the noveaux riches. Living in the Spring Garden neighborhood had become a status symbol. In October 2000, the Philadelphia Historical Commission reported that, of the 1,400 homes that existed in the Spring Garden District, about half of them were built before 1860, when Parry and Randolph were most active.

In 1854, Oliver Parry and Nathaniel Randolph built a residence for Nathaniel at 1709 Green Street. That was later the location of the "Bush Hill Sanitorium," established in 1914 at 1709 to 1711 Green Street. In 1917, Dr. Anderson founded the Anderson Hospital there. It was later named College of Physio-Therapy in 1920, when it included 1707 to 1713 Green Street.[40] The building was altered in 1922 and again in 1988.

Like Nathaniel Randolph, many of the developers of the Spring Garden District also resided in the neighborhood. Josiah Haines resided at 1716 Green Street, just across the street from Nathaniel Randolph. Haines's brother, Clayton, was a bricklayer who lived at Twenty-Third and Green Streets. Carpenters Hiram Miller and Samuel Coulson resided at 2211 and 2134 Green Street, respectively.

Nathaniel Randolph's Home at 1709 Green Street
Photograph by Stephen T. Krencicki

2100 Block of Mount Vernon Street Looking West
Photograph by Stephen T. Krencicki

2100 Block of Mount Vernon Street Looking East
Photograph by Stephen T. Krencicki

The Panic of 1857 was felt around the world and to some extent in Philadelphia. Oversupply and reduction in demand for American grain due in most part to the end of the Crimean War, and a dramatic increase in manufacturing that far outpaced the demand for its products, helped to bring it on. Numerous British investors removed funds from the nation's banks, casting grave doubts about the overall soundness of the US economy. The growing confusion over the state bank note system capped by the failure of the Ohio Life Insurance and Trust Company in August 1857 sparked the panic. In that year the stock market declined by 66 percent. More than five thousand American businesses failed. The country did not recover until 1859.

By 1860 the population of Philadelphia had climbed to more than 565,000 people. The panic appears to have created much concern for Oliver Parry in his drive to develop his Spring Garden properties. A letter that he had written to his sons Edward and Richard on November 11, 1857, vividly describes the financial crisis that existed at that time and the actions that Parry was taking to confront it. Oliver writes:

> Much care will be necessary to avoid difficulty; as the disastrous state of affairs in the east will assuredly reach the west in a greater or lesser degree and I want you to be prepared for the worst. We hope the worst is over here, but there is very little perceptible improvement in anything ... Our business is pretty much confined to furnishing lumber for our own buildings which are getting pretty well advanced—we are urging them forward as fast as possible knowing that if they had to be sold unfinished there would be a great sacrifice made on them ...
>
> I remain your affectionate
> Father

Four months later in March 1858, Edward and Richard's uncle, Richard Randolph, wrote to them from Philadelphia congratulating them on their good fortune in Minnesota (his nephews had founded a bank in Mankato, Minnesota):

You speak of six percent a month for money as a mighty little affair. What a pity you have not got a million to put out on such like terms … I'll tell you what I am willing to do, if you encourage me to do it—I will try to furnish one or two thousand dollars for you to invest in good securities … so as to make up some of my losses here …

Your affectionate Uncle,
Richard

Nathaniel Randolph died in his residence at 1709 Green Street on Friday, September 4, 1858, after suffering from a horrific case of cholera. He was only forty-one years old. After his death, the responsibility for the operation of the extensive Parry and Randolph businesses fell on the shoulders of Oliver Parry to manage. Parry described his melancholic state of mind at "your cousin Nathaniel's death" to his sons, Edward and Richard, in a letter that he had written to them in September 1858. Maintaining his business sense, he asked his sons to confirm that "the five hundred dollars that Nathaniel has left each of you has been deposited into your bank accounts." Nathaniel's relative, Edwin T. Randolph, continued the family trade after Nathaniel's death. He resided at 1730 Mount Vernon Street.

Spring Garden Neighborhood Was Home to Noted Entrepreneurs and Professionals

As the Spring Garden neighborhood's attractiveness and popularity grew, it drew more of Philadelphia's elite developers and professionals. The Philadelphia City Directory of 1866 reported that six of twelve physicians in the city were based on Green Street, indicating the high regard for the neighborhood with its wide tree-lined streets. Thomas Cowperthwait Eakins, one of the most noted artists in the history of American art and arguably the most popular hometown artist in Philadelphia history, resided at 1729 Mount Vernon Street. Eakins was a realist painter and sculptor who painted hundreds of portraits of friends and family and featured some of the most prominent people in Philadelphia society in his works.

The preeminent manufacturer of fine hats, John B. Stetson, built his home at 1717 Spring Garden Street. S. F. Whitman, the famous chocolatier who gave chocolate lovers the "candy map" so they knew what they were getting, lived at 1701 Spring Garden Street. Pittsburgh Plate Glass magnate John Pitcairn Jr., made his home at 1634 North Sixteenth Street. Unfortunately, that building has been demolished.

The construction of the United States Mint at Sixteenth and Spring Garden Streets, now part of the Community College of Philadelphia, was supervised by the renowned architect, Amos Boyden, who lived at 2210 Mount Vernon Street. Boyden was also a charter member of the Art Club of Philadelphia. The residence of Robert Purvis, the devoted antislavery activist, was located at 1601 Mount Vernon Street, where it is said that he had hidden escaping slaves. Wills Eye Hospital was the first institution in the United States that was devoted to the care of eyes. John Wills, a Quaker merchant, left an endowment to fund the hospital. The original institution was built at Seventeenth and Spring Garden Streets in 1832. Wills Eye Hospital was designed by revered Philadelphia architect John T. Windrim. He also designed the Franklin Institute and the Philadelphia Municipal Court buildings on the Benjamin Franklin Parkway, the Thomas Jefferson Medical College and Hospital, and the Research Institute at Lankenau Hospital among many other architecturally splendid buildings.

Oliver and Rachel Parry circa 1835
Courtesy of the New Hope Historical Society

Rachel Randolph Parry

Rachel, born on November 6, 1804, was the youngest child of Edward Fitz Randolph. He dropped the name Fitz after the war. He was a partner with Josiah Langdale Coates in the prestigious Philadelphia shipping firm known as Coates & Randolph. Edward married Anna Juliana Steel when she was just seventeen years old, and they had thirteen children. His son, Jacob Randolph, MD, married Sarah Emlen Physick, daughter of the eminent Philadelphia physician, Philip Syng Physick, MD, the "Father of American Surgery." Ironically, as a young physician just out of medical school during the outbreak of the yellow fever epidemic, Dr. Physick volunteered his services at the hospital established in the Bush Hill area of Philadelphia. That was the location where Rachel's husband, Oliver, would develop into an extensive residential area about sixty years later.

In 1797, Dr. Physick returned to the Bush Hill hospital to assist the sick and dying victims of the epidemic when it ravaged the city once again. Dr. Physick convinced Rachel's brother, Jacob, to leave his general practice to become a surgeon. Jacob Randolph graduated from the University of Pennsylvania School of Medicine in 1830. From 1835 until his tragic and untimely death in 1848 he was a surgeon at Pennsylvania Hospital. He became a lecturer on clinical surgery at the University of Pennsylvania in 1843 and a professor in that branch in 1847. It was Dr. Jacob Randolph who selected the epitaph for Dr. Philip Syng Physick: "He gave his honours to the world again. His beloved part to heaven and slept in peace."[41]

Dr. Jacob Randolph and his wife, Sarah, moved into Dr. Physick's house at 321 S. Fourth Street in the city after his death and, soon after, they added a wing to the north side of the building. Their country seat was located in Fairmount Park and was known as the Randolph House. It is also known as Laurel Hill. The mansion had originally been built by Francis Rawle, a Loyalist, who had much of his property confiscated after the American Revolutionary War. Dr. Physick purchased the home in 1828. It was passed on to the Randolphs after his death. They added the octagonal addition to the home sometime after 1830. The Randolphs entertained many of Philadelphia's famous residents, including the author James Fenimore Cooper. Is it possible that they could have discussed the fact that James Fenimore Cooper's grandfather,

James Cooper, had once owned land in the Manor of Moreland that later belonged to the Parry family? The Randolphs were regarded as wonderful hosts, and many of the old Philadelphia families who maintained summer residences in that area were lavishly entertained by them. Numerous distinguished guests from all walks of life were feted in the spacious halls of residences like the Randolph House.

The Physick House
Photograph by Stephen T. Krencicki

Dr. Jacob Randolph's death by drowning ended a brilliant medical career. He was only fifty-two years old. He left behind his beloved wife and three children. His daughter, Elizabeth, married Louis Wister. His twin sons, Samuel and Philip, were both admitted to the Philadelphia bar. His wife, Sarah (Sally), outlived all of their children. The city of Philadelphia acquired the Randolph House in 1869 and included it in Fairmount Park. It was restored by the generous contributions of the Philadelphia chapter of the Colonial Dames of America around 1900. The Women for the Bicentennial, later the Women for a Greater Philadelphia, restored the house in 1976 and continued to maintain it. In his family records in March 1901, Richard Randolph Parry referred to the home as "Uncle Jacob Randolph's country seat." The Randolphs' home on South Fourth Street is now occupied by the Philadelphia Society for the Preservation of Landmarks and is open for public tours.

Although Rachel was the youngest of thirteen children, her and Oliver's twelve children contributed generously to the family's already-burgeoning family tree. In the mid- and late-nineteenth century in Philadelphia and New Hope, in whatever direction one would turn, it seemed most likely that one would find a Parry or Randolph involved in one business or profession or another.

Rachel's father was an incorporator of Philadelphia National Bank and was a member of the Philadelphia City Council in 1794. As early as 1813, Edward Randolph had purchased property and five contiguous frame dwellings on the block between Mulberry (now Arch) Street and Filbert Street (now John F. Kennedy Boulevard) on the west side of Twentieth Street from Anthony Cuthbert and John Jones. Oliver and Rachel Randolph Parry also owned two properties on that block. Edward and his family resided at 212 North Second Street and later at Thirteenth and Master Streets in the city. Rachel's mother died suddenly on February 11, 1810, leaving her husband a widower with ten children. Edward Randolph died in 1837 at the age of eighty-three and was interred in "Friends Grounds" at the corner of Sixteenth and Race Streets in Philadelphia. He is said to have left a considerable fortune.

Even before Oliver Parry and Nathaniel Randolph began to develop the western extension of Philadelphia around the area formerly known as Bush Hill, they and their families had become directly involved in improving the social fabric of that part of the city. Oliver was a life member of the Philadelphia City Institute that was organized in 1852 to establish a free library for the residents of Philadelphia. Rachel Randolph Parry and Rachel's sister, Julianna Randolph, became charter members of the Western Association of Ladies for the Relief and Employment of the Poor in 1846.

Rachel was a member and Julianna was the first treasurer, and she and Rachel were members of the Acting Committee. Parry family records show that Julianna had inherited a number of properties on Poplar Street in the Northern Liberties District of Philadelphia and another at what is now the northeast corner of Twenty-Second and Market Streets from her father, Edward Randolph, in 1851. The role of the committee members was to visit applicants for work at the House of Employment. They conducted home visits for that purpose. The association "devised means for the relief and employment of the suffering and deserving poor of the western part of the city."[42] The difficulty of procuring employment and the enormous price of fuel, high rents, and high markets were all taking a widening toll on the city's poor families. The association opened a House of Employment in that same year, which furnished relief to 165 women and children.

In 1854, the association glowingly reported that "from the garrets of our great city, from its cellars too, those sepulchers in which the living lie! Unsunned, unaired, unvisited and unwarmed—their lonely occupants come forth, to be cheered, comforted, morally elevated and instructed in our bright and cheerful Work Room. Soon it became a cherished home to them.… In conformity with rules relative to personal cleanliness, long indulged habits of self-neglect, gradually give place to comparative neatness." The women were instructed in plain sewing, and their children were placed in a nursery on South Sixteenth Street, where a person was provided to take care of them. This appears to have been one of the first job-training and child-care programs in the history of Philadelphia and of the young nation. It set a new standard for services to the poor.

The number of applicants to the association's various relief programs continued to grow, and in 1855, they were already petitioning to purchase a plot of ground to erect a suitable building to address the growth in demand for their services. The records for the association show that the

Parry and Randolph families were also financial contributors to the programs. Nathaniel Randolph donated to the Shoe Fund and was a subscriber. The association donated 202 pairs of shoes to the poor that year and appealed to its members for additional donations because of the growing need that had been demonstrated by poor families in the city at the time. Julianna Randolph, Rachel Randolph Parry, Oliver Parry, Oliver and Rachel's daughter Julianna Parry, and their son Richard Randolph Parry were also subscribers. Records show that, at the time, the Parry family resided at 633 Arch Street in Philadelphia, and the Randolphs lived at 674 Chestnut Street in the Old City area. Notably, in addition to their work as volunteers, both families contributed financially to the association. The annual bylaws also indicate that the association had established a form of bequest for the donation of funds and property in wills.

Julianna Randolph continued to support the association for the rest of her life. She passed away on August 28, 1876. In her will she bequeathed one thousand dollars to their programs. She also demonstrated her commitment to the poor families of Philadelphia by leaving funds for the Association for the Care of Colored Orphans, the Home for Colored Children near the Woodland Cemetery, and the Old Man's Home of Philadelphia.

The Western Association of Ladies for the Relief and Employment of the Poor became a major force, providing social and educational services for the disadvantaged families in Philadelphia in the second half of the nineteenth century. They built their House of Employment at 19 South Seventeenth Street, and it was located there for several decades. That is now the site of the One Liberty Place Building, which is home to one of the city's finest men's clothing shops.

The association noted in their annual report of 1855 that 109 women were employed there. They also cared for thirty children in their nursery. The production report for that year showed an output from those employed that included eight hundred garments, two hundred comfortables (quilts or comforters), twenty silk skirts, and ten large bed quilts. The fabric and materials for the products were donated by residents, churches, and businesses. These items were sold at the association's store, which was located at 10 South Sixteenth Street. The total receipts for the year of 1855 were $2,685.41.[43] This represented an increase of nearly 20 percent over the previous year and was quite a sizable amount of funds when compared to today's economy. The association later added a Visiting Housekeepers Bureau, expanding the types of assistance that they were providing to the poor families in Philadelphia.

When Rachel died in 1866, the association noted her passing in its twentieth annual report that reflected upon her dedicated service:

> It is with saddened hearts that we enter upon our duties this coming season, for we have been sorely stricken. One who has ever been in the foremost ranks, has been taken from us, taken from a life of usefulness, with a heart alive to sympathy and sorrow; and a hand ever open to freely give; pleasant and cheerful in her address, and amiable and kind to all. These endearing qualities made the presence of our dear friend, Rachel Parry, ever welcome; welcome to the young, whom she so cordially assisted with her advice and council, and welcome to those more advanced in life, for her good judgment and her readiness to assist and sustain.
>
> She has borne the "burden and the heat of the day" in this society, being one of the few among us who were its earliest members, has nursed it in its infancy, and with an interest unchanging, was a faithful worker until she was called away from works to reward.
>
> One of the strong pillars has been removed from among us; may her example be an incentive to those who follow after, and then, "although dead, she yet liveth."
>
> Hannah Ann Zell, Secretary
> Officers of the Western Association of Ladies for the Relief and Employment of the Poor
> 20th Annual Report
> November 1, 1866
> Philadelphia, Pennsylvania

The heartfelt reference to Rachel Randolph Parry is a testimony to her spirit of kindness and diligent work for the less fortunate in Philadelphia at a time when poverty was rampant in the city. The association in which she was an early and vital active member continues its work in Philadelphia today, nearly 150 years after her death.

Oliver Parry died on February 20, 1874, in his town home at 1721 Arch Street in Philadelphia. He was laid to rest at the Solebury Friends Burying Ground in Bucks County, Pennsylvania, just outside New Hope. His townhome was sold to William T. Taylor, and as has been noted, it was demolished in the latter part of the twentieth century to accommodate the construction of the mammoth Bell Atlantic/Verizon Tower that now soars over the once-humble Quaker neighborhood on Arch Street between Seventeenth and Eighteenth Streets. The expansive Quaker enclave had at one time stretched along Arch Street from Fourth to Twentieth Streets.

The value of Oliver Parry's estate in today's economy would be well over five million dollars. In his will he bequeathed a generous sum of cash and a townhome to each of his eight surviving children. Richard Randolph Parry inherited 1614 Mount Vernon Avenue; Jane Parry Winslow, 1616 Mount Vernon Avenue; Edward Randolph Parry, 1618 Mount Vernon Avenue; Emma Randolph Parry, 2122 Mount Vernon Avenue; Helen Randolph Parry, 2124 Mount Vernon Avenue; Jane Parry Winslow, 2132 Mount Vernon Avenue; Mary Randolph Richardson, 2134 Mount Vernon Avenue; and George Randolph Parry inherited 2144 Mount Vernon Avenue. In addition to these residences, the children were bequeathed shares in rents from grounds located at Bodine Street near Columbia Street, Clayton Street east of Twenty-Third Street, the west side of Phillips Street south of Diamond Street, Clayton Street west of Twenty-Second Street, the southeast corner of Norris and Mercer Streets, and the southwest corner of Norris and Mascher Streets.[44] The entire city block encompassing the homes of 2102 to 2144 Mount Vernon Street remains in use today in one of Philadelphia's most peaceful and serene neighborhoods.

Oliver Parry's obituary published in the *Philadelphia Inquirer* beautifully reflected on his most productive and decent life:

This gentleman, though retired for many years from the busy walks of life, was, in his day, a most active and useful citizen, and to his and to his nephew and partner, the late Nathaniel Randolph, the city of Philadelphia is indebted for the fine improvements made on Green and other streets in "Bush Hill" in the north-western section of the city, they having purchased much of the ground in that section, and either had it improved for themselves or sold land to others, whom they induced to have buildings erected upon it, the result being the conversion of what was once a barren waste or vast gullies, into one of the handsomest and most attractive neighborhoods of which Philadelphia can boast of at the present day.

Born a member of the Society of Friends, he lived and died in that faith, walking through life with a singleness and direct honest of purpose which made the name of Oliver Parry synonymous with truth and honor.

At the close of a long and well spent life he rests from his labors and is at peace, his soul having gone, we have every assurance, back to the God who gave it. Long will he be missed and long will he be remembered by the near ones whom he has left behind to mourn his loss, and who will keep the fragrant recollection of his memory green for themselves and their children's children.

The Philadelphia Inquirer
February, 1874

CHAPTER 5
The Parry Legacy

M ore than 225 years have passed since young Benjamin Parry established himself in New Hope and helped to catapult the town into prominence as the manufacturing and industrial capital of Bucks County, Pennsylvania. He was the driving force that brought new prosperity to a town that was just beginning to come into its own. He led the way in the construction of the first bridge. He spearheaded the establishment of the town's first commercial bank, and he was in the forefront of those who set out to expand the industrial footprint of the growing community. His patented grain-drying invention helped farmers throughout the young country to expand their overseas markets. He was active in the construction and financing of the Delaware Canal that vastly enhanced the transportation network in Pennsylvania and New Jersey. Nearly one hundred buildings that were built during the Parry era remain in use today. Parry's flour mill had been incorporated into the legendary Bucks County Playhouse when it was established in 1939. His barn now houses an upscale import shop, and his home remains the gleaming jewel of architecture in New Hope as the headquarters of the town's historical society.

Benjamin Parry's son, Oliver, and Oliver's nephew, Nathaniel Randolph, led the way in Philadelphia more than a century and a half ago in expanding the city's grid westward. They developed boulevards, cozy streets, and hundreds of charming townhomes in an area that just a few years before had been the site of a barren wasteland full of vast gullies.

Today, most of the housing development in the city of Philadelphia takes the form of vertically stacked, compartmentalized structures of concrete, glass, and steel. Many of Oliver Parry's row houses along the tree-lined streets of the Spring Garden neighborhood remain as residential oases amid the gleaming high-rise towers of Center City.

Oliver Randolph Parry
Portrait by David E. Kornhauser circa 1913
Courtesy of the New Hope Historical Society

Oliver Randolph Parry

At the turn of the twentieth century, the population of Philadelphia exploded in unprecedented growth. The number of people living in the city skyrocketed by more than 650,000 in the first 30 years of the twentieth century to a total of 1,950,000 residents. Hundreds of thousands of immigrants from Europe joined many thousands of African Americans from the southern states who were streaming into the city. Housing again became scarce and overcrowded. Streets were widened, and boulevards connecting segments of Philadelphia were constructed.

Oliver Parry's grandson, Oliver Randolph Parry, enhanced his family's legacy in Philadelphia. He began his career in the city amid its rapid and unparalleled growth. His business pursuits in the city stretched from the latter part of the nineteenth century until well into the twentieth century. His father, Richard Randolph Parry, was one of the pioneers of Minnesota in Territorial days and took part in bringing the subsequent state into the union. As we saw earlier, Richard was a founder of the Mankato Bank in Minnesota and was heavily involved in land speculation along the proposed routes of the railroad expansion in the Midwest, including Nebraska, Minnesota, and Iowa. Later he became the family's unofficial historian as he continued to gather family documents and correspondence that, fortunately, have been preserved by the New Hope Historical Society and the Spruance Library in Doylestown, Pennsylvania.

Richard continued correspondence with a family relative, Francis Parry, who had lived in London but traveled to the United States frequently. Francis was heavily involved in British politics and assisted Richard with his efforts to document the Parry family pedigree. During that time Francis was attempting to be named British commissioner to the Chicago World's Fair and was a frequent traveler to Washington DC. In a revealing letter to Richard Randolph Parry in December 1890, Francis Parry described the deteriorating condition of the fabled Willard Hotel in the nation's capital: "This hotel is just so horrid, a lot of semi-toughs of both sexes, and the place overheated to suffocation; most slovenly writing room, must hide in one's bedroom."

Shortly after the letter had been written by Parry, the old Willard Hotel—whose guest lists included many US presidents, including

Abraham Lincoln—was demolished. The new hotel was rebuilt on the site and opened in 1904. Today the magnificent Willard InterContinental Hotel, with its vast office complex, exhibits historical artifacts from its colorful history, including a copy of Abraham Lincoln's hotel bill in the amount of $773.73, which, it is said, was paid with funds from his first paycheck as the sixteenth president of the United States.

After completing his early education from a tutor and later at Saint Luke's School in Wayne, Pennsylvania, and at the Bordentown Military Institute in New Jersey, Oliver Randolph Parry enrolled in the University of Pennsylvania's class of 1896, although he did not complete his degree there. Just a couple of years later, he was known as a building designer and later had been listed as an architect. Parry was a partner in the firm of Witmer and Parry in the early part of his career. Parry had already completed several projects by the time he was twenty-five years old. Listings of Parry's projects had been included in the *Philadelphia Record and Builders Guide* around 1905, and in 1909 the city directory listed the office of his architectural firm located at 1723 Chestnut Street, just half a block west of what is now the location of the One Liberty Place high-rise building. His growing popularity and the wide success of his varied projects required additional office space, and he later moved his office to 1524 Sansom Street. For a brief time, Oliver resided at 1604 Pine Street. Parry had one child, a daughter, Margaret Parry Lang, with his first wife, Lida Mae Kraemer. Lida Mae, a former New York City chorus girl, died in 1944 and is buried in the Morris Cemetery in her hometown of Phoenixville, Pennsylvania.

Philadelphia Architects and Buildings reports that, at the peak of his career, Oliver Randolph Parry maintained offices in Philadelphia and New York City, and he was president and director of the Bay Court Estates Company in Great Neck, Long Island. He was also known to have been the architect for several New York and New Jersey companies. Parry designed a significant number of industrial buildings using reinforced concrete materials. Some of his notable buildings that demonstrated the wide diversity of his work were the Protestant Episcopal Missions in Chestnut Hill, the Bucks County Country Club, the Atwold Country Club, the Old York Road Country Club (now demolished), and the T. J. Stewart High School in Norristown, Pennsylvania, a suburb of

Philadelphia. It continues to serve the Norristown community today after having been converted into their middle school in 1973.

Parry was selected in 1908 as architect and supervisor of construction for the design of apartment buildings and other structures that were built on fifteen acres located on Lansdowne Avenue in Darby, Pennsylvania, a suburban Philadelphia community, on the site formerly known as the Joshua L. Bailey Estate and later as the J. C. Wilson Estate. In the same year, Parry was commissioned by the Wilkie Brothers to prepare the plans and specifications for the construction of eighty-four dwellings and stores that were to be built on the southeast corner of Fifty-Fourth Street and City Avenue at a cost of $400,000. That was the site of the old Black Horse Hotel, which was, according to Parry's notes, to be demolished to accommodate the massive development. It appears, however, that the project was never constructed. Today the land is part of the prominent Saint Joseph's University campus.

Parry designed and built a large, modern dairy in what is known as the Brewery Town neighborhood of Philadelphia on Twenty-Sixth Street between Jefferson and Oxford Streets in Philadelphia for the Wills-Jones-McEwen Company in 1913. He boasted that the design of the building paid special attention to economy in construction, space, and operation. His goal was to provide economy for future maintenance. He used reinforced concrete and cage frame, with walls and partitions of brick covered with cement. Nearly one hundred years later, Parry's structure houses one of the largest private electrical contracting firms in the city of Philadelphia. In New Jersey, he built additions to his alma mater, the Bordentown Military Institute, and later designed a movie theater in Cape May, New Jersey, which was a popular summer getaway for the Parry family for generations.

When Oliver Randolph Parry was selected to plan and design the addition to the James A. Welsh School in Norristown, Pennsylvania, in 1914, the president of the school board, Mr. McCarter, was quoted praising Parry as "the most capable man ever employed by the school district of Norristown along the lines of architectural work."

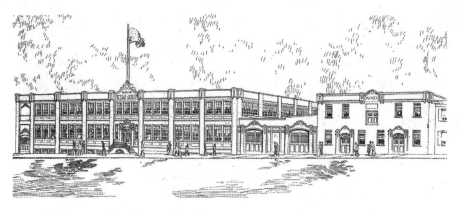

Parry's Design for the Willis-Jones, McEwen Company Dairy in 1913
Courtesy of the New Hope Historical Society

Parry served overseas with distinction in World War I, attaining the rank of captain. He was assigned to the US Army Corps of Engineers and was a member of both the Military Order of the Loyal Legion of the United States and the Military Order of the World War. He later served as captain of D Company, 304th Engineers, (Combat) Organized Reserves, 79th Division. He remained very active in the American Legion and was at one time commander of the Taylor E. Walthour (later Ingersoll Walthour) post number 282. After completing his service to the country in the war, Parry returned to Philadelphia to continue his architectural pursuits. Prior to the beginning of his career in Philadelphia, he had been head of the firm of E. P. Gardner and Company in Scranton, Pennsylvania.

Oliver Randolph Parry was one of the original supporters of the design and construction of the proposed Benjamin Franklin Parkway. He championed the right of the city of Philadelphia to control the character of structures that were to be built and would line the new boulevard. The parkway and the expansion of Roosevelt Boulevard provided convenient links to the western part of Philadelphia and to its suburban communities.

The wealthier families gravitated to the suburbs in Montgomery and Bucks Counties as the center of the city became vastly overcrowded. Parry built residences for B. C. Giles in Haverford, S. J. Buxton in Saint David's, F. A. Willis in Gwynedd, and Reginald H. Morris in Villanova—all in suburban Philadelphia. Perhaps the Morris residence underscores best Oliver Randolph Parry's intrepid passion for the expanded use of concrete in the construction of homes. It was a two-story and attic dwelling in the mission style that was built entirely of solid reinforced concrete. It was topped by a red Spanish tile roof and decorated with red concrete terraces and white concrete walls.

Parry designed twelve residences for Worrall and Wilkinson in Kennett Square and twenty-four residences for the Reading Railroad Line near Glenside, Pennsylvania. His company also designed the National Bank in Berlin, New Jersey, and the National Bank in Collegeville, Pennsylvania. He received widespread notoriety for his design of the large sanitary concrete dairy that was constructed on North Twenty-Sixth Street between Jefferson and Oxford Streets in Philadelphia.

The *Who's Who in Philadelphia* publication in1926 listed Oliver Randolph Parry as an architect, author, and orator. One of his later and most extensive projects was completed in 1927 for the All-Ken Company that included a theater, a bank, stores, and an arcade located near Germantown Avenue and Hunting Park Avenue in Philadelphia.

Unlike his grandfather, Oliver, and his great-grandfather, Benjamin, Oliver Randolph Parry's travel between New Hope and Philadelphia was not limited to the long and cumbersome Old York Road. In March 1891, after numerous attempts to establish a railroad link between the two towns, the Northeast Pennsylvania Railroad Company's first steam train departed the New Hope depot bound for Philadelphia.[45] The first locomotive was the Chestnut Hill 300, a Baldwin locomotive formerly owned by the Philadelphia, Germantown, and Norristown Railroad.[46] At last, a trip from Philadelphia that for centuries required a full day of rough-and-tumble travel was reduced to a comparatively comfortable two hours. Railroad transportation was gradually extended from Philadelphia toward New Hope. So his grandfather, Oliver Parry, may have used the railroad to as far as Hatboro, less than fifteen miles from New Hope. Oliver Randolph Parry followed the example of his father, using the new means of transportation for the entire trip. He also rode the Philadelphia–Camden ferry on his trips to New Jersey.

On June 15, 1907, Oliver's father had given the relatively new rail line one of its greatest publicity venues when he traveled from Philadelphia with about 250 members of the Pennsylvania Society of the Sons of the American Revolution. The group arrived at what is now known as the New Hope & Ivyland Railroad Station and marched about two blocks to the Parry Mansion. There, on the back lawn of his grandfather's home, Richard Randolph Parry and the Sons of the American Revolution commemorated the evacuation of the British troops from Philadelphia. Parry led the ceremonies with his historic address titled "Coryell's Ferry in the Revolution," in which he advocated changing the town's name back to Coryell's Ferry to honor its historic place in the Revolutionary War. Although he continued to promote the idea, the suggestion was never adopted.

At its peak the New Hope rail line offered as many as twenty trains each day. In addition to the passenger service, the railroad provided a vital transportation system for farmers in New Hope and Bucks County. It was one of the busiest milk routes in the entire railroad system that included about ten thousand miles. Most of the products were shipped on the New Hope branch, and their destination was the Reading Terminal in Philadelphia where the Reading Terminal Market continues to be a major Philadelphia attraction. Today the New Hope & Ivyland Railroad continues to run between New Hope and Lahaska with a depot located just a few hundred yards from the Buckingham Friends Meeting House and Elm Grove, the former Paxson estate.

Far more so than the previous Parry generations, Oliver Randolph Parry was a member of and participant in a wide variety of clubs and organizations in the Philadelphia community. The *Philadelphia Architects and Buildings* noted that, for several years, he had written articles about architecture and engineering in New York and Philadelphia newspapers. In July 1914, the American Concrete Institute published Parry's paper titled "The Artistic Treatment of Concrete Structures," in which he took his industry to task for its lack of interest in the use of concrete as a building material. He advocated for the increased publicity of the artistic treatment of concrete in construction. Parry enjoyed drawing buildings and landscapes. His sketchbook of local Bucks County, Pennsylvania, and New Jersey scenes is preserved in the archives of the New Hope Historical Society. He also authored stories in magazines about historical events and is author of *Betsy Ross and the United States Flag*. He enjoyed lecturing on topics, including history, genealogy, military, and civic affairs.

Parry married Carmita de Solms Kennedy on October 11, 1928,

at the Second Presbyterian Church at Twenty-First and Walnut Streets in Philadelphia. They resided at 2211 Locust Street in the fashionable Rittenhouse Square neighborhood of the city and were very active in the community social scene. Oliver's cousin, Jean Maule, resided just around the corner at 2217 Rittenhouse Street. Carmita, born in Bryn Mawr, Pennsylvania, was a very talented artist whose works were displayed at the Pennsylvania Academy of Fine Arts and at the Philadelphia Sketch Club. Her talent as a writer was evident in the portfolio of numerous romantic poems that she had written. Carmita completed writing courses with the Home Correspondence School of Springfield, Massachusetts. Her writing style is clearly revealed in the following excerpt from her short story that she wrote around 1924 titled "Ocean City, New Jersey." The beach resort on the Atlantic Ocean was a favorite summer playground for Philadelphians then, and it still is today.

> The heart of the mariner on his way down the coast to the fabled Indies, throbs with a touch of homesickness as he sees the glow of the myriad lights of Atlantic City painted upon the evening sky. Like the blaze of a great conflagration it spreads upwards and outwards in a huge fan-shaped illumination. At the southern end there is a break, as though Midas, drawing his fingers across the horizon, had lifted them for a moment and then had pressed more lightly. Under the fainter light lies Ocean City, at the extremity of Peck's Beach.

Carmita was active in the Plays and Players Club, the Philadelphia Art Alliance, the Genealogical Society, and the Navy League. Carmita was president of the Saint Agnes Hospital Auxiliary for many years and was a member of the board of directors of the Women's College Hospital. Oliver was a member of the Philadelphia Art Alliance, the Pennsylvania Society of the Sons of the American Revolution, the Penn Athletic Club, the Pen and Pencil Club, the Concrete Institute, and the Plays and Players Club.

Oliver was an original member of the Old York Road Country Club. He and Carmita were known to have been contributors to a number of charitable causes in Philadelphia, including the Philadelphia Museum of Art, to which several of Carmita's paintings had been bequeathed. In April 2008, the museum's board of trustees sold a beautiful set of Chinese export porcelain circa 1790 that had been donated by the Parrys to benefit the museum's acquisitions funds.

Parry's social involvement was such that it prompted a writer for Philadelphia's *The Evening Ledger* in April 1915 to comment that "architect, author and multi-clubman Oliver Randolph Parry is so popular he has had a beverage named after him—The Parry Toddy. He belongs to nearly everything and knows nearly everybody."

Regents Row in New Hope
Photograph by Roy Ziegler

After a long and brilliant career in Philadelphia and a sustained role as one of the city's most prominent socialites, Oliver Randolph Parry retired to his boyhood home at the Parry Mansion in New Hope following the death of his wife, Carmita, in 1938. Ever the architect, he set about designing a new kitchen addition for the home that provided modern conveniences for himself and his two sisters then living at the eighteenth-century mansion. After his retirement, he continued to write and pursue public speaking. Parry died peacefully in his sleep at the Parry Mansion on April 22, 1958, in his eighty-fifth year. His only remaining sister, Adelaide, died within a few days after his death. The *New Hope Gazette* on April 24, 1958, remembered him as "a proud and colorful figure and his death marks the end of an era. Typical of his rectitude was his refusal to accept a government pension due him as a veteran. Typical, too, was his modesty with regard to the name of our borough. New Hope was known as Coryell's Ferry when his ancestors bought the Hope Mill here in 1784."

The Parry Mansion in 2010
Photograph by Roy Ziegler

Margaret Parry Lang, Oliver Randolph Parry's only child, moved back into her childhood home in New Hope in 1966 from her residence in Honey Brook, Pennsylvania, a small town in Chester County that was about the same size as New Hope, after she had inherited the Parry Mansion from the Parry Estate. Her generous cooperation and that of her husband, Oliver Paul Lang, with the New Hope Historical Society made it possible for the organization to purchase the home and preserve and renovate the Parry Mansion for the edification and enjoyment of the public. The home has continued to be available for public tours since the completion of the renovations in 1973, and it preserves Parry family documents in its archives. There visitors can learn about the outstanding legacy of the Parrys as they tour the eighteenth-century Georgian-style residence that was home to five generations of the Parry family. The varied architecture of the town representing three centuries of rich history, its passion for the arts, and its preserved natural beauty contributes to New Hope's reputation as the top tourist destination in the county today.

The Spring Garden Neighborhood in 2010
Photograph by Stephen T. Krencicki

By the early part of the twentieth century, many of the homes that Oliver Parry had constructed in Philadelphia were subdivided to provide residences for the growing population. Some of the smaller housing units that were created in the subdivisions housed more than a dozen people. Under the watchful eye and support of the city, many of the homes have been restored and preserved.

Today, in the Spring Garden neighborhood of the city of Philadelphia, scores of the townhomes that Oliver Parry had built, and hundreds more whose construction he inspired more than 150 years ago, continue to provide comfortable residences. Their gardens line the shady streets that Parry and Randolph helped design and develop in the middle of the nineteenth century. The National Register of Historic Places pays homage to those homes today in the twenty-first century, and the legacy of the Parry family lives on in Philadelphia in the heart of one of the city's most serene and picturesque neighborhoods.

Notes

1. Parry family records
   Benjamin Parry files
   New Hope Historical Society

2. British Towns and Villages Network
   History of Caernofonshire
   July 2009

3. "A History of Willow Grove" written for schools and community
   Willow Grove Guide, October 1975, Section 15

4. "A Synopsis of the History of Moreland Township and Willow Grove"
   Joe Thomas, Upper Moreland Historical Society, p. 26

5. *The Tavern at the Ferry*
   Edwin Tunis
   The Johns Hopkins University Press, 1973, p. 26

6. Parry family records
   Benjamin Parry files
   New Hope Historical Society

7. *Architectural Patterns in an Early River Town*
   Margaret Bye Richie, PhD
   University of Pennsylvania, 1987, p. 76

8. *Asylum "A Paris in the Wilderness"*
   Rebecca Geoffroy

9. History of Wayne, Pike and Monroe Counties
   Alfred Mathews, 1886, p. 820

10. Francis Curley papers
    New Hope Historical Society, p. 3

11. *The Difference Began at the Footlights: A Story of Bucks County Playhouse*
    Gilda Morigi, 1973, p. 32

12. *Waking Giant: American in the Age of Jackson*
    David S. Reynolds
    HarperCollins, 2008, p. 85

13. Parry family records
    Benjamin Parry files
    New Hope Historical Society

14. Parry family records
    Benjamin Parry files
    New Hope Historical Society

15. Letters of patent to Benjamin Parry
    Benjamin Parry files
    New Hope Historical Society

16. Francis Curley papers
    New Hope Historical Society, p. 4

17. *History in the Making*
    May, 2006, p. 6
    New Hope Historical Society

18. *Philadelphia Merchant: The Diary of Thomas P. Cope*
    Edited by Eliza Cope Harrison
    South Bend, Indiana
    Gateway Editions Limited, 1978, p. 285

19. Parry family records
    Benjamin Parry files
    New Hope Historical Society

20. Parry family records
    Spruance Library, MSC-429, File 3
    Doylestown, Pennsylvania

21. Biddle's Philadelphia Directory, 1791

22. Parry family papers
    Spruance Library, MSC-259, File 1
    Doylestown, Pennsylvania

23. Parry family papers
    Spruance Library, MSC-259, File 1
    Doylestown, Pennsylvania

24. Parry family papers
    Spruance Library, MSC-259, File 2
    Doylestown, Pennsylvania

25. Parry family records
    Different lots of land of B. Parry, AD 1828
    Spruance Library, MSC-429, File 3
    Doylestown, Pennsylvania

26. *History of Bucks County Pennsylvania: From the Discovery of the Delaware to the Present Time*
    W. W. H. Davis
    Democrat Book and Job Office Print
    Doylestown, Pennsylvania
    1876, p. 738

27. Solebury Township
    Bucks County, Pennsylvania
    John Richardson
    Offset Service Company, Philadelphia, Pennsylvania
    December, 1958, p. 43

28. *Old Roads Out of Philadelphia*
    John T. Faris
    J. B. Lippincott & Company, 1917, p. 259

29. *Willow Grove Spirit*
   M. Whitehead

30. Pennsylvania Society of Colonial Dames
   June 1920

31. *Buckingham Friends Meetinghouse: A Brief History of the Meeting House of Buckingham*
   February 2010, p. 2

32. Parry family records
   Oliver Parry files
   New Hope Historical Society

33. *Avenue One: Atlases of Philadelphia*
   Bryn Mawr University, p. 6

34. Parry family records
   Oliver Parry files
   New Hope Historical Society

35. *Philadelphia: A 300-Year History*
   Russell F. Weigley, Editor
   W. W. Norton & Company, 1982, p. 185

36. Girard College
   History
   Elizabeth Laurent, Director of Historical Resources

37. Brief of title to various lots of ground, part of the Bush Hill Estate, the property of Oliver Parry and Nathaniel Randolph
   E. K. Price, Esq., 1858, p. 26

38. Philadelphia Historical Commission
   Spring Garden Historic District
   October 2000, p. 181

39. Heath House, Schooley Mountain Springs
    New Jersey
    J. Warren Coleman, Manager
    1880, p. 4

40. Philadelphia Historical Commission
    Spring Garden Historic District
    October 2000, p. 74

41. *Dr. Physick and His House*
    George B. Roberts
    "The Pennsylvania Magazine of History and Biography"
    January 1968, pp. 84–86

42. Preamble, Charter, and By-laws of the
    Western Association of Ladies for the Relief and Employment of the Poor
    T. Ellwood Zell, Publisher, 1869
    Urban Archives, Samuel Paley Library
    Temple University, Philadelphia, Pennsylvania, p. 1

43. "Report of the Board of Managers of the Western Association of Ladies
    for the Relief and Employment of the Poor, 1855"
    Urban Archives
    Samuel Paley Library
    Temple University, Philadelphia, Pennsylvania, p. 8

44. Parry family records
    Oliver Parry files
    New Hope Historical Society

45. New Hope & Ivyland Railroad
    New Hope to Lahaska Narration
    February, 2010, p. 2

46. Solebury Township, Bucks County
    John Richardson
    Offset Service Company, Philadelphia, Pennsylvania
    December 1958, p. 52

Index